# Study Guide, Vol. 1

# The Earth and Its Peoples

## A Global History Advanced Placement* Edition

FOURTH EDITION

Richard W. Bulliet / Pamela Kyle Crossley / Daniel R. Headrick / Steven W. Hirsch / Lyman L. Johnson / David Northrup

**Bill Strickland**

*East Grand Rapids High School*

HOUGHTON MIFFLIN COMPANY BOSTON NEW YORK

Publisher: *Suzanne Jeans*
Senior Sponsoring Editor: *Nancy Blaine*
Senior Marketing Manager: *Katherine Bates*
Editorial Assistant: *Adrienne Zicht*
Editorial Assistant: *Paola Moll*
New Title Project Manager: *Susan Peltier*



Printed in the U.S.A.

ISBN 13: 978-0-618-78921-4
ISBN 10: 0-618-78921-9

123456789–POO–11 10 09 08 07

# Contents

CHAPTER 1

# From the Origins of Agriculture to the First River-Valley Civilizations, 8000–1500 B.C.E.

## BEFORE YOU BEGIN

This chapter is important for two reasons: (1) it models the kinds of questions one asks in historical inquiry; and (2) it gives the basic information on early civilizations that you'll use for comparing to the information in later chapters. As you read, look for common *patterns* among the chapter's sections on prehistoric, Mesopotamian, Egyptian, and Indus civilizations, but don't try to memorize every pharaoh and king or worry too much about precise dates. You should be able to place events in the correct chronological *order* and correct *century*, but you will not need to place events into a specific year.

## LEARNING OBJECTIVES

After reading Chapter 1 and completing this study chapter, you should be able to:

- Explain how geography and climate interact with the development of human society, including demographic factors.
- Place the major agricultural, technological, political, and cultural developments in this chapter in the correct time period.
- Evaluate the appropriateness of using "civilizations" as the basic unit of historical study.
- Give cultural and technological examples of diffusion, and compare them to examples of independent invention.
- Compare the political, cultural, and social characteristics of ancient Mesopotamia, Egypt, and Indus Valley civilizations.

## IDENTIFICATIONS

Define each term and explain why it is significant, including any important dates.

**Paleolithic**

______________________________

______________________________

**foragers**

______________________________

______________________________

**Neolithic**

______________________________

______________________________

**agricultural revolutions**

**Çatal Hüyük**

**civilization**

**Babylon**

**Sumerians**

**Semitic**

**city-state**

**Hammurabi**

**scribe**

**cuneiform**

**irrigation**

**Nubia**

**pharaoh**

**pyramid**

**hieroglyphics**

**papyrus**

**Harappa**

**Mohenjo-Daro**

**"systems failure"**

## MULTIPLE-CHOICE QUESTIONS

Read the entire question, including *all* the possible answers. Then choose the *one* answer that best fits the question.

1. Naturalists first surmised that humans originated in
   a. Europe.
   b. Africa.
   c. Asia.
   d. America.
   e. Australia.

2. Why is the name "Stone Age" misleading?
    a. It implies that people lived in stone dwellings.
    b. People used tools made out of many things, not just stone.
    c. People used tools made only of bone.
    d. Stone tools have been used throughout all of human history.
    e. People did not use stone tools during this time.
3. Which of the following traits does *not* describe hunting and gathering bands?
    a. The bands could be of any size.
    b. The bands must have had enough people in them to adequately provide for themselves.
    c. The bands must have remained highly mobile to follow herds.
    d. Men usually hunted.
    e. Women usually gathered.
4. Which of the following was *not* fundamental to the success of agriculture?
    a. Good tools
    b. Long-distance trade
    c. Permanent settlements
    d. Slash-and-burn techniques
    e. High-yield strains of plants
5. Agriculturalists produced more specialized material goods and art than hunter-gatherers because
    a. hunter-gatherers didn't trade and thus had no market for which to produce a surplus of material goods.
    b. farmers had more free time than hunters and gatherers did.
    c. agricultural societies had more sophisticated tastes.
    d. they were able to record how to make such things as pottery, jewelry, and metal goods using newly invented writing systems.
    e. larger communities of people could spare some members from food production for more specialized activities.
6. Which of the following attributes is *not* essential to the modern definition of civilization?
    a. A codified legal system
    b. Specialization of labor, and many people involved in nonfood production
    c. Monumental buildings
    d. A system for keeping permanent records
    e. Major advances in the sciences and arts
7. The peoples of ancient Mesopotamia tended to see the world as a hazardous place because
    a. their gods were inaccessible.
    b. the Tigris and Euphrates Rivers tended to flood unpredictably.
    c. of the constant warfare in their region.
    d. of the corruption of their government.
    e. of the scarcity of resources.
8. The successful operation of large-scale sophisticated irrigation systems generally depended on
    a. plentiful rainfall to justify such an expenditure of energy.
    b. the emergence of individuals or groups capable of compelling and organizing large numbers of people to work together.
    c. tremendous communal cooperation, usually led by local village councils.
    d. the importation of advanced technology and sometimes even of foreign workers.
    e. the ability to produce written diagrams and instructions.

9. Many Mesopotamian states engaged in warfare mainly because
   a. they needed to gain access to raw materials through force.
   b. their religion demanded it.
   c. they constantly needed to defend their territory.
   d. warfare was a rite of passage that proved a young man's virility.
   e. they enjoyed it.
10. Why do we know so little about women in ancient Mesopotamia?
    a. Women were illiterate.
    b. Women were unimportant in Mesopotamian society.
    c. It was forbidden to discuss women in public.
    d. Male scribes tended to write about elite male activities.
    e. We know little about anyone in Mesopotamian society.
11. Which of the following best characterizes changes in women's status in the transition from hunting and gathering to agricultural societies?
    a. Women lost social standing and freedom.
    b. Women gained power and wealth.
    c. Women became less important in the public realm but more important in the sacred world.
    d. Women became less important in the sacred world but more important in the public realm.
    e. Women's status did not change.
12. What commodity did Mesopotamia possess in abundance?
    a. Gold
    b. Silver
    c. Bronze
    d. Camels
    e. Clay
13. In Egypt, the ebb and flow of successful and failed regimes seemed to be linked to
    a. trade.
    b. the cycle of floods.
    c. annual rainfall.
    d. the activity of surrounding peoples.
    e. astronomical events.
14. Our ability to read ancient Egyptian writing is due to
    a. the work of computer linguists.
    b. Howard Carter's unearthing of Tutankhamun's tomb.
    c. the discovery of the Rosetta Stone.
    d. the fact that Egyptians today can still read it.
    e. the fact that the text has yet to be deciphered.
15. What circumstances led to Egypt becoming a focal point of civilization?
    a. Outside conquest
    b. Internal turmoil
    c. Climatic change
    d. Famine
    e. Both climatic change and famine

16. Which of the following about Egyptian slavery is *not* true?
    a. It existed only on a limited scale.
    b. Slaves were often prisoners of war.
    c. Slaves were often debtors or criminals.
    d. Treatment of slaves was relatively humane.
    e. Slaves were never freed.
17. Egypt's interests abroad focused primarily on
    a. conquest of territory.
    b. acquisition of new slaves.
    c. accumulating new technologies.
    d. maintaining access to valuable resources.
    e. intimidating their many enemies.
18. Why have the Indus stone seals *not* provided historians with a clear picture of Indus society?
    a. No one can read them.
    b. Indus peoples used riddles to confuse their enemies.
    c. The stone seals were not used for writing but for decoration.
    d. Indus peoples used stone seals only to write about people outside their own civilization.
    e. The seals were only used in bookkeeping, never for historical records.
19. Indus society can best be described as
    a. mostly urban.
    b. rural.
    c. imperial.
    d. nomadic.
    e. despotic.

## ESSAY QUESTIONS

Make an outline for each question, listing the major points you want to discuss. Then write your practice essay, following your outline carefully and making sure that you do not skip any of your major points. At this time, you will want to add the relevant dates and details that will make your essay persuasive and accurate.

### Change Over Time

There really aren't any COT questions relevant yet. There needs to be more *time* for change to happen. This will be an important part of later chapters, but it's still too premature.

### Compare and Contrast

1. Compare and contrast the likely social, religious, and economic characteristics of a hunter-gatherer society to residents of a Neolithic town like Çatal Hüyük.

2. Compare and contrast the advantages and disadvantages in using "civilization" as the basic unit of historical study.

3. Compare the political, social, and cultural characteristics of Mesopotamia, Egypt, and Indus Valley civilizations.

## COMPARISON CHARTS

Using information gathered from the text, fill in the blank areas of each chart with the relevant data pertaining to the regions and categories listed. (Not all blank areas will necessarily be equally complete.)

**Chart 1.1 Prehistoric to Neolithic Society**

| Characteristic | Hunter-gatherer society | Neolithic town |
|---|---|---|
| Social Structure | | |
| Religious Practices | | |
| Economic Activity (Including Technology) | | |

| Chart 1.2 Early River Valley Civilizations | | | |
|---|---|---|---|
| **Characteristic** | **Egypt** | **Mesopotamia** | **Indus Valley** |
| Social Structure | | | |
| Cultural Accomplishments | | | |
| Political Structure | | | |

## DIVERSITY AND DOMINANCE

After reading "Diversity and Dominance: Violence and Order in the Babylonian New Year's Festival" in your text, answer the following additional questions.

1. What is the significance of taking the scepter, circle, and sword from the king, and then returning them later?
2. What was the role of the priest in the New Year's Festival?
3. How powerful were the priests and why?
4. What does it mean when Marduk defeats Tiamat? Why is it significant that he uses her body to create sky and land?

## INTERNET ASSIGNMENT

**Keywords:** **Egyptian hieroglyphics**

**cuneiform**

**Indus seals**

Egyptian and Sumerian writings represent some of the earliest forms of writing in the ancient world. Try to imagine a world before writing—it's difficult for modern people because writing is so much a part of our world. But in ancient times, only a few people knew how to write, and writing had very specific uses. Use the above keywords to find websites about ancient forms of writing. You might want to consult the *History WIRED* image library on the Bulliet, *The Earth and Its Peoples* website (refer to the preface of this study guide for information on how to locate the Bulliet home page).

1. Who knew how to read and write in ancient societies?
2. What was writing used for?
3. How do the writing systems of Egypt, Sumeria, and the Indus Valley differ?
4. Where do scholars find ancient writings today, and what can they tell us about ancient worlds?
5. What can we not learn from these writings and why?

## INTERNET EXPLORATION

When people think of the ancient Egyptians, they think of mummies. Scholars too have benefited from the study of mummies and tombs. Look up the keywords "Egyptian mummification," and see what Egyptologists do every day.

Two specific sites you may like are http://www.ancienthistory.about.com/education/ancienthistory/library/howto/ht_mummy.htm?rnk=r&terms=mummies and http://www.nationalgeographic.com/media/tv/mummy.

1. How difficult was the process of mummification?
2. What does this tell us about death in ancient Egypt?
3. Did mummification depend on social class?
4. How do modern scholars study mummies, and what is done to preserve them?

## MAP EXERCISES

On Outline Map 1.1, shade in these ancient river civilizations:

Mesopotamia

Egypt

China

India

Then plot Jericho and Çatal Hüyük.

On Outline Map 1.2, mark the land of Mesopotamia. Then plot the following:

Tigris River

Euphrates River

Ashur

Sumer

Uruk

Babylon

On Outline Map 1.3, mark the region of Egypt. Then plot the following:

Nile River

Upper Egypt

Lower Egypt

Upper Nubia

Lower Nubia

Giza

## Outline Map 1.1

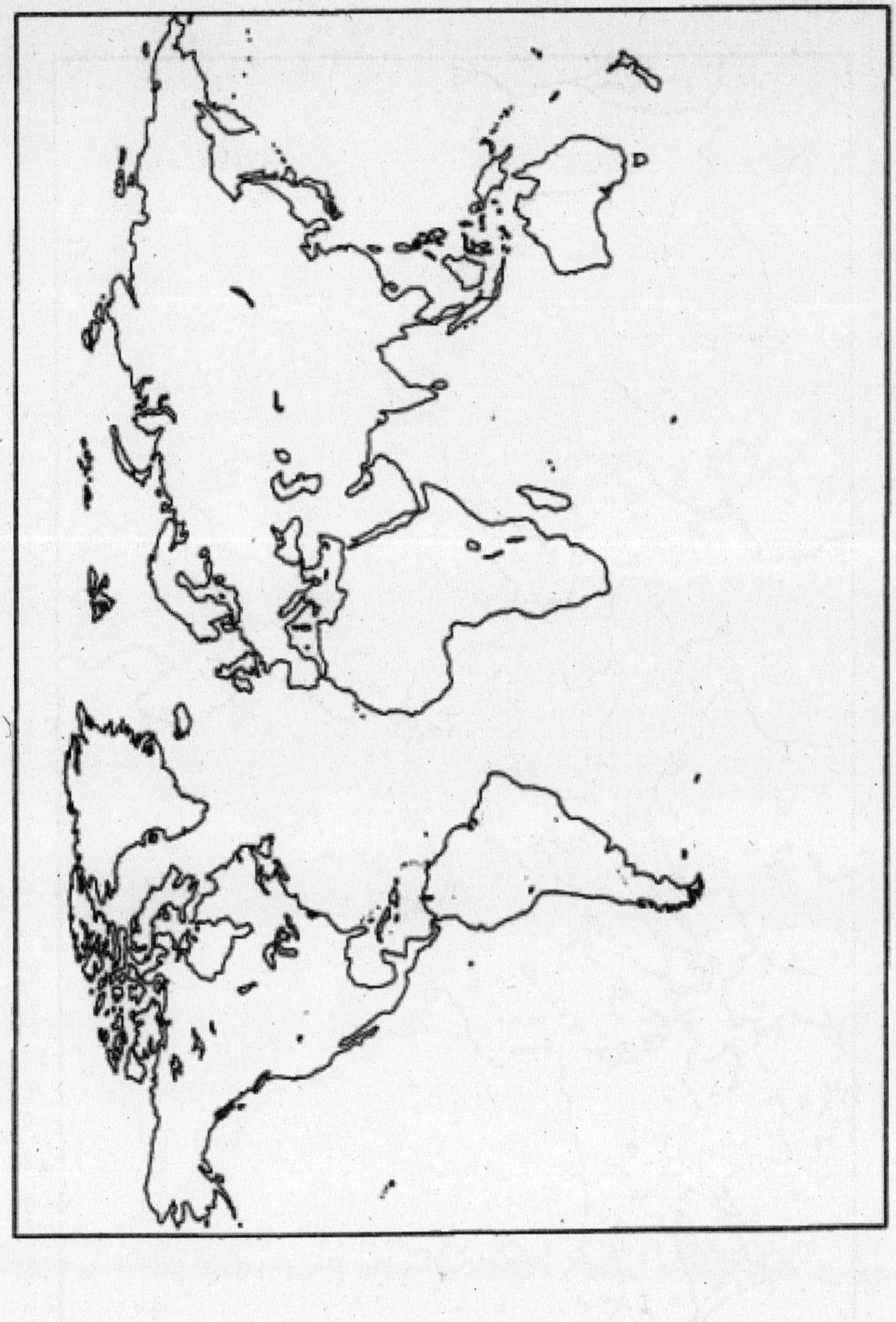

## Outline Map 1.2

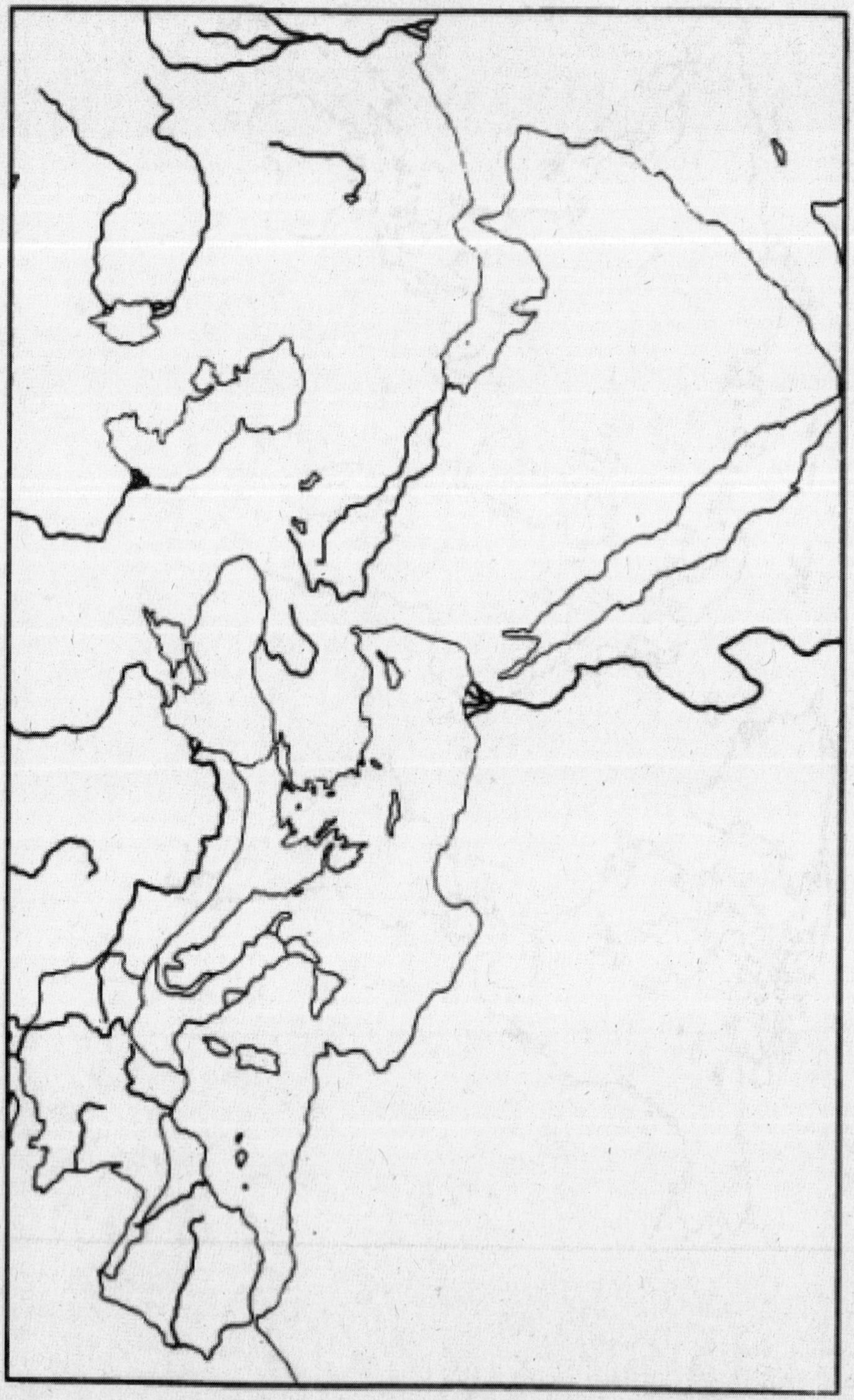

## Outline Map 1.3

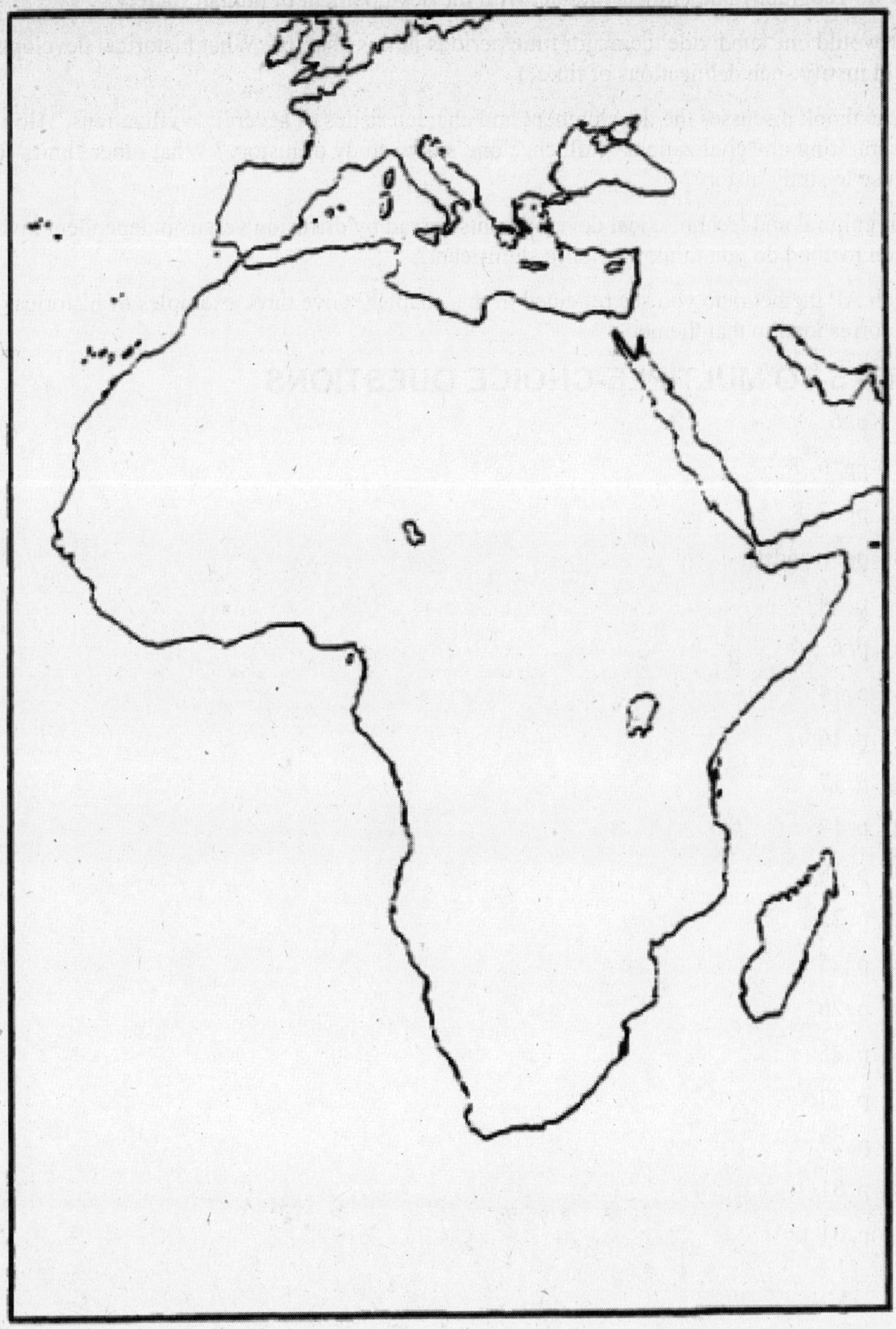

## FOCUS QUESTIONS

1. How do geography and climate interact with the development of human society?
2. How would one subdivide the major time periods in this chapter? What historical developments would justify such delineations of time?)
3. The textbook discusses the development and characteristics of several "civilizations." How might concentrating on "civilizations" influence one's own study of history? What other "units" could one use to study history?
4. What cultural and technological developments spread by diffusion versus independent invention? Which method do you think was more significant?
5. Which AP theme(s) do you see reflected in this chapter? Give three examples of historical events that correspond to that theme.

## ANSWERS TO MULTIPLE-CHOICE QUESTIONS

1. c p. 6
2. b pp. 6–7
3. a pp. 7–8
4. b pp. 8 and 10
5. e p. 14
6. a p. 6
7. b p. 14
8. b p. 16
9. a p. 17
10. d p. 18
11. a p. 18
12. e p. 23
13. b p. 25
14. c p. 26
15. c p. 25
16. e p. 27
17. d p. 27
18. a p. 31
19. a p. 31

CHAPTER 2

# New Civilizations in the Eastern and Western Hemispheres, 2200–250 B.C.E.

## BEFORE YOU BEGIN

Like Chapter 1, this chapter models the kinds of questions one asks in historical inquiry and presents the basic information on early civilizations that you'll use for comparing to the information in later chapters. By the end of this chapter you'll know the basic information about all major regions around the world. As you read, look for common *patterns* in Chinese and American civilizations, but don't try to memorize every example or worry too much about precise dates. You should be able to place events in the correct chronological *order* and correct *century*, but you will not need to place events into a specific year.

## LEARNING OBJECTIVES

After reading Chapter 2 and completing this study chapter, you should be able to:

- Give cultural and technological examples of diffusion, and compare them to examples of independent invention.
- Compare the political, cultural, and social characteristics of ancient China and American civilizations.
- Compare the teachings/philosophies of Legalism, Confucianism, and Daoism.

## IDENTIFICATIONS

Define each term and explain why it is significant, including any important dates.

**Loess**

________________________________________

________________________________________

**Shang**

________________________________________

________________________________________

**bronze**

________________________________________

________________________________________

**"barbarians"**

________________________________________

________________________________________

**divination**

**Zhou**

**Son of Heaven**

**Mandate of Heaven**

**yin/yang**

**Legalism**

**Confucius**

**Daoism**

**Kush**

**Olmec**

**Chavín**

**oracle bones**

______________________________________________

______________________________________________

## MULTIPLE-CHOICE QUESTIONS

Read the entire question, including *all* the possible answers. Then choose the *one* answer that best fits the question.

1. Shang authority was demonstrated by
   a. the happiness of the people.
   b. the size of urban centers.
   c. ritual sacrifice.
   d. the possession of horses.
   e. the possession of cast bronze vessels for sacrifices to the gods.
2. Which of the following technologies was *not* developed by the end of the Shang dynasty?
   a. Monumental royal tombs
   b. The horse-drawn chariot
   c. Writing
   d. Gunpowder
   e. Trade networks
3. In the Zhou period, the separation of religion from political dealings allowed China to
   a. make war on its neighbors.
   b. develop important secular philosophies.
   c. abandon all religious practices.
   d. adopt Buddhism.
   e. discontinue human sacrifice.
4. Confucius used the term *ren* to mean
   a. benevolence toward all humanity.
   b. benevolence toward the family only.
   c. nonviolence.
   d. female subservience.
   e. the Mandate of Heaven.
5. Which of the following is an example of independent invention in the first millennium B.C.E.?
   a. Development of fire in Nubia
   b. Spread of matriarchy in Olmec society
   c. Use of irrigation technology during the Zhou dynasty
   d. Development of bronze metallurgy technology
   e. Creation of Confucian concept of *ren*.
6. Where was Kush?
   a. In the Nile Delta
   b. In the fertile plain of Dongola Reach
   c. Celtic Europe
   d. Kush was the Egyptian name for China.
   e. Kush was an alternate name for Egypt.

7. Which of the following issues did Confucianism and Legalism, but *not* Daoism, address?
   a. Familial relationships
   b. Veneration of ancestors
   c. Role of the afterlife in political decisions
   d. Political relationship between ruler and ruled
   e. Role of religious clergy in society
8. Why did the Nubian peoples enter the historical record?
   a. They became advanced enough to be considered a legitimate society.
   b. They came in contact with the literate peoples of the Mediterranean.
   c. They developed writing.
   d. They won the war against the Macedonians.
   e. The Druids adapted the Latin alphabet to the Celtic language.
9. Which of the following is *not* a way in which Nubian women differed from their Middle Eastern or Greek and Roman counterparts?
   a. Celtic women participated equally with men in warfare.
   b. Celtic women occasionally served as queens of their tribes.
   c. Celtic women had greater sexual freedom.
   d. Celtic women had the right to inherit the family estate.
   e. Celtic women sat at banquet and helped solve vexing problems.
10. Most scholars think that the American continents have
    a. had frequent contact with all other continents over the last ten thousand years.
    b. been virtually isolated from the rest of the world for the last fifteen thousand years.
    c. been frequently visited by peoples from Asia.
    d. been frequently visited by peoples from Africa.
    e. not had any contact with outside peoples since it was first settled.
11. Mesoamerica was never unified
    a. politically.
    b. economically.
    c. religiously.
    d. culturally.
    e. technologically.
12. The Olmec can be described as
    a. a mystery culture—leaving little evidence and no legacy.
    b. ruling over a great empire.
    c. a great military power.
    d. the first civilization of Peru.
    e. never having an empire but influencing regions by controlling commodities such as jade.
13. Which of the following statements about llamas is *not* true?
    a. Llamas were first domesticated in Venezuela.
    b. Llamas were the only domesticated beasts of burden in the Americas.
    c. Llamas were similar in their role in South America to that of camels in the trans-Saharan trade.
    d. Llamas facilitated trade.
    e. Llamas provided meat and wool.

## ESSAY QUESTIONS

Make an outline for each question, listing the major points you want to discuss. Then write your practice essay, following your outline carefully and making sure that you do not skip any of your major points. At this time, you will want to add the relevant dates and details that will make your essay persuasive and accurate.

### Change Over Time

There really aren't any Change Over Time questions relevant yet. There needs to be more *time* for change to happen. This will be an important part of later chapters, but it's still too premature.

### Compare and Contrast

1. Compare and contrast the appropriateness of Confucianism, Legalism, and Daoism in creating a stable society.
2. Compare the political, cultural, and social characteristics of ancient Chinese and American civilizations.

## COMPARISON CHARTS

Using information gathered from the text, fill in the blank areas of each chart with the relevant data pertaining to the regions and categories listed. (Not all blank areas will necessarily be equally complete.)

| Comparison Chart 2.1 | | | |
|---|---|---|---|
| | **Legalism** | **Confucianism** | **Daoism** |
| Founder (and Approximate Date) | | | |
| Summary of Basic Teachings | | | |
| View of Human Nature | | | |
| Ideal Government | | | |
| Advantages / Strengths | | | |
| Disadvantages / Weaknesses | | | |

**Chart 2.2 Early Civilizations, part 2**

*(Be sure to reference to Chart 1.2 Early River Valley Civilizations)*

| Characteristic | China | Americas | |
|---|---|---|---|
| Social Structure | | | |
| Cultural Accomplishments | | | |
| Political Structure | | | |

| What are each society's major characteristics in each category? | Mesopotamia | Egypt | India | China (Shang and Zhou) | Americas |
|---|---|---|---|---|---|
| Political Structure and Philosophy | | | | | |
| Economic Basis | | | | | |
| Social Structure | | | | | |
| Gender Roles | | | | | |
| Religion | | | | | |

## DIVERSITY AND DOMINANCE

After reading "Diversity and Dominance: Hierarchy and Conduct in the Analects of Confucius" in your text, answer the following additional questions.

1. How do you think Confucius viewed the individual's place in society? Does this attitude extend to all members of society—does even the ruler have responsibility?
2. What do you think about the statement: "The Superior Man seeks within himself. The inferior man seeks within others"? Who is the Superior Man, and what is his role in Confucian society?

## INTERNET ASSIGNMENT

**Keywords:** **megaliths**

**Olmec heads**

The European megaliths, like Stonehenge, and the Olmec heads are two examples of large stone works. Use the above keywords to find websites about European megaliths and Olmec heads. You might want to consult the *History WIRED* image library on the Bulliet, *The Earth and Its Peoples* website (refer to the preface of this study guide for information on how to locate the Bulliet home page).

1. How do megaliths and Olmec heads differ in appearance and use in society?
2. How were they made and transported? Explore the various theories. Which theories seem the most reasonable?

## INTERNET EXPLORATION

The discovery of oracle bones in China over one hundred years ago proves that history can change. What new things has that discovery taught us? Recently more oracle bones have been discovered. Use the keywords "oracle bones" to check out the old and new discoveries.

## MAP EXERCISES

On Outline Map 2.1, mark the extent of the Shang dynasty and the Zhou dynasty. Also, trace the winter monsoon winds and summer monsoon winds.

On Outline Map 2.2, shade in the Olmec homeland and the Chavín state.

## Outline Map 2.1

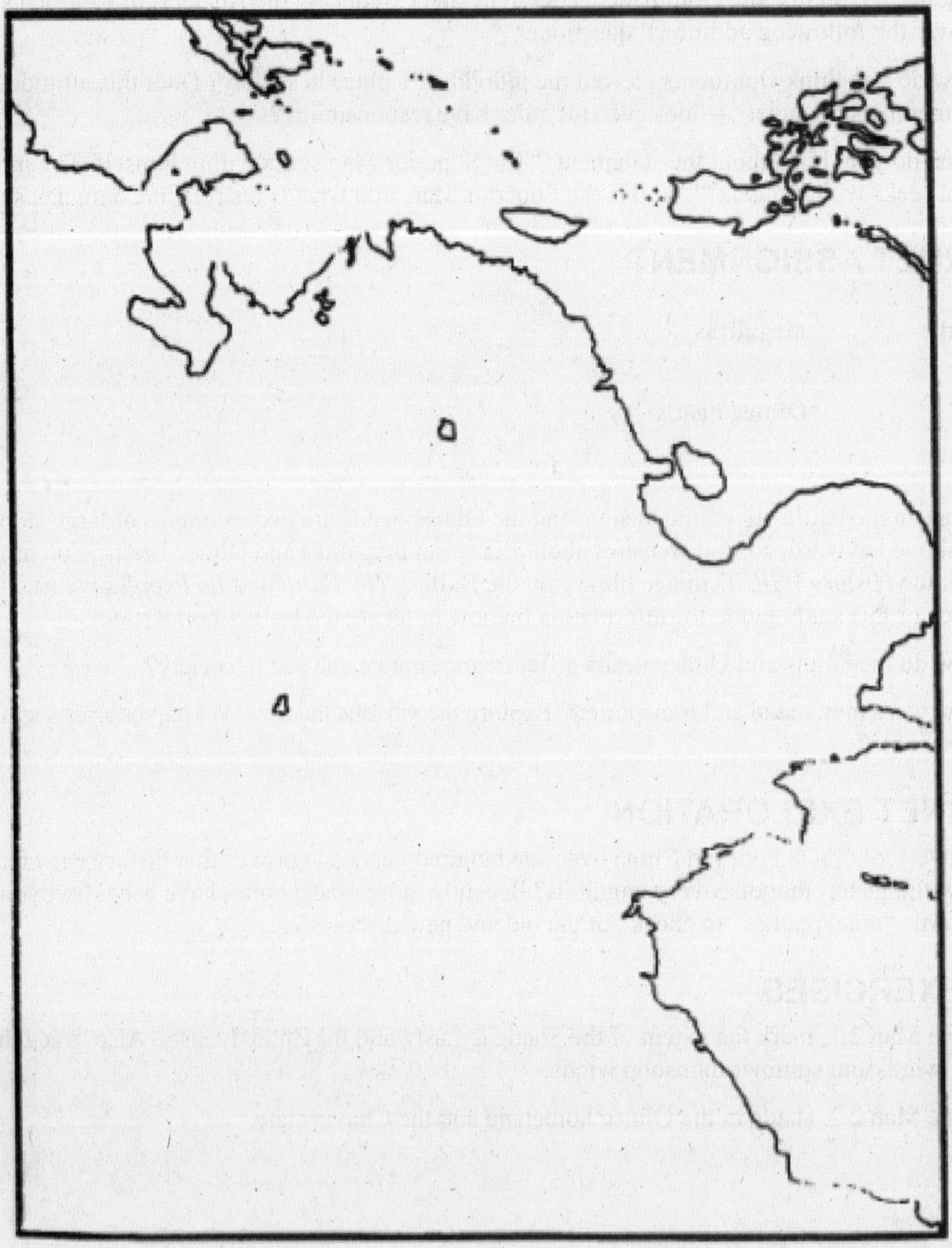

## Outline Map 2.2

## FOCUS QUESTIONS

1. How do ancient societies compare in their political, cultural, and social structure? Which was more significant in creating similarities among ancient societies, diffusion or independent invention?
2. How do the teachings of Legalism, Confucianism, and Daoism compare?

## ANSWERS TO MULTIPLE-CHOICE QUESTIONS

1. e p. 44
2. d p. 44
3. b p. 46
4. a p. 47
5. d p. 51
6. b p. 52
7. d p. 50
8. b p. 52
9. a pp. 53–54
10. b p. 54
11. a p. 55
12. e p. 57
13. a p. 58

CHAPTER 3

# The Mediterranean and Middle East, 2000–500 B.C.E.

## BEFORE YOU BEGIN

The Foundations time period can be subdivided into two sections: Ancient (prior to 1000 B.C.E.) and Classical (1000 B.C.E. to approximately 500 C.E.). This chapter wraps up the "ancient" time period. As you read, look for patterns common to all ancient civilizations and compare the characteristics described in this chapter to earlier civilizations. In a few chapters you'll need to compare earlier ancient civilizations to later classical civilizations.

## LEARNING OBJECTIVES

After reading Chapter 3 and completing this study chapter, you should be able to:

- Explain how the environment may have influenced the development of the peoples of the Mediterranean and Middle East.
- Explain how the early Iron Age was a time of migration of large numbers of people and what impact those migrations had on the land and peoples of that period.
- Explain how land-based and sea-based empires differed from each other in style, technique, and philosophical outlook.
- Explain what new complex political, social, and economic structures evolved in the era of empire building.
- Discuss the unique contributions of the Phoenician and Hebrew civilizations.

## IDENTIFICATIONS

Define each term and explain why it is significant, including any important dates.

**Iron Age**

______________________________________________

______________________________________________

**Hatshepsut**

______________________________________________

______________________________________________

**Akhenaten**

______________________________________________

______________________________________________

**Ramesses II**

**mass deportation**

**Israel**

**Hebrew Bible**

**First Temple**

**monotheism**

**Diaspora**

**Phoenicians**

**Carthage**

**Neo-Babylonian kingdom**

## MULTIPLE-CHOICE QUESTIONS

Read the entire question, including *all* the possible answers. Then choose the *one* answer that best fits the question.

1. Which of the following was *not* helpful to the success of the Hittite Kingdom?
   a. Horse-drawn chariots
   b. Rich deposits of copper, silver, and iron
   c. The ability to forge iron tools
   d. The discovery of the lost wax method for casting bronze
   e. The adaptation (and simplification) of cuneiform to their language
2. *Hyksos* means
   a. Terrible Invaders.
   b. Benevolent Rulers.
   c. the People.
   d. the Noble People.
   e. Princes of Foreign Lands.
3. Which of the following is *not* true about the relationship between Egypt and Nubia?
   a. Nubia served as a buffer zone against invasion.
   b. The Egyptians placed forts and garrisons of Egyptian soldiers in Nubia.
   c. The Egyptians pressed the Nubian population to adopt Egyptian language and culture.
   d. The Egyptians deported the Nubians to Assyria.
   e. The Egyptians extracted tribute from the Nubians.
4. How did the Egyptians respond to Hatshepsut's rule?
   a. They were opposed to the concept of having a woman as a ruler.
   b. They welcomed such an able ruler.
   c. They never knew she was the actual ruler because she always claimed to rule through her son as her regent.
   d. They never knew she was a woman because her portraits always showed her wearing a beard.
   e. They feared her because they thought she was a sorceress.
5. What was Akhenaten's motivation in modifying the Egyptian religion to emphasize the primacy of Aten (the sun)?
   a. He wanted to bring Egyptian religion more in line with other religions in the Middle East.
   b. He believed that worshipping the sun would increase agricultural production.
   c. He was attempting to reassert the superiority of the pharaoh and to renew belief in his own divinity.
   d. He hoped that by disillusioning the people he could make them abandon religion altogether and become better workers.
   e. He wanted to undermine the popularity of the new Isis cult.
6. What was the source of the rivalry between Egypt and the Hittite Kingdom?
   a. The question of who would rule the world
   b. Control of the trade routes in Syria-Palestine, the region lying between them
   c. Defining their mutual border
   d. The rich agricultural lands of Mesopotamia
   e. Control of Nubian gold

7. Which of the following did *not* encourage the inhabitants of the Aegean islands to commence seafaring?
   a. Limited arable land
   b. Frequent flooding of their farmlands
   c. Scarcity of resources
   d. Natural harbors
   e. Rocky and arid land
8. What can scholars *not* prove about the relationship between the Minoans (Cretans) and the Mycenaeans?
   a. Crete controlled the mainland.
   b. Mycenaeans borrowed the idea of the palace and pottery.
   c. Mycenaeans borrowed the idea of a centralized economy and administration.
   d. Greek culture is made up of a mix of peoples from Crete and Mycenae.
   e. Mycenaeans borrowed the idea of writing.
9. The annihilation of the major trading partners and disruption of trade routes
   a. helped bring about the end of Mycenaean civilization, thus illustrating the degree to which the major centers of the Late Bronze Age were interdependent.
   b. disrupted the Mycenaean economy in the short term.
   c. caused the merchants to demand equal voting rights.
   d. caused Mycenae to invade Crete.
   e. had no effect on the Mycenaean centers.
10. Which was the first real empire in world history?
    a. Mesopotamia
    b. Egypt
    c. Assyria
    d. China
    e. Rome
11. Why did the rulers of the Neo-Assyrian military follow the trade routes in their campaigns?
    a. The caravans were an excellent source of booty.
    b. The roads were good.
    c. They could disguise themselves as traders.
    d. By controlling the trade routes, they blocked all entry into Assyria.
    e. Due to the breakdown of the international economy, the roads were deserted.
12. What made possible the Assyrians' conquest of their empire?
    a. Their tolerance for the desires of their subjects
    b. Their military organization and technology
    c. Their superior manufacturing and trade networks
    d. Their religious system for legitimating rule
    e. Propaganda
13. In Assyria, the term *human beings* referred to
    a. all people of the empire.
    b. ethnic Assyrians only.
    c. military and civil elites only.
    d. all peoples of the world.
    e. the royal family only.

14. The text of the Hebrew Bible (Old Testament) best reflects the view of the
    a. fifth century B.C.E. priests who controlled the Temple of Jerusalem.
    b. twelve apostles.
    c. prophet Abraham.
    d. medieval Christian monks who compiled both the Old and New Testaments from the Hebrew and Greek texts.
    e. Roman conquerors.
15. Which of the following was *not* among King David's innovations in his plan to strengthen Israel?
    a. He built a great wall all around his kingdom to repel invaders.
    b. He captured Jerusalem and made it his capital.
    c. He brought the Ark of the Covenant to Jerusalem.
    d. He took a census and collected taxes.
    e. He maintained a strong standing army.
16. Because of its lack of land, the Phoenician civilization concentrated on
    a. waging wars to acquire more land.
    b. religious pursuits.
    c. trade and manufacturing.
    d. hiring themselves out as mercenaries.
    e. academic pursuits.
17. Why do historians know more about Carthage than they know about the Phoenician homeland?
    a. The Phoenicians developed writing only after establishing Carthage.
    b. Roman and Greek records tell more about Carthage than other Phoenician city-states.
    c. When the Persians took over the eastern Mediterranean, they burned all the old Phoenician records.
    d. Carthage was simply more important throughout time than any other Phoenician city.
    e. Historians don't know any more about Carthage than any of the other Phoenician cities.
18. Textile production has generally been the preserve of women because
    a. it was easy and undemanding.
    b. it was possible to care for children and spin or weave at the same time.
    c. men's hands are too large and clumsy to work with textiles.
    d. women are more fashion-conscious.
    e. goddesses were often associated with spinning and weaving.
19. What do historians consider Phoenicia's most significant long-term cultural contribution to world history?
    a. Their navigational technology and sophisticated map-making skills
    b. Impressive trade networks linking Persia to the eastern Mediterranean
    c. Their development of writing based on an alphabet
    d. Their political philosophy that encouraged equal roles for women in policy decisions
    e. Religious practices that allowed the worship of only one god

# ESSAY QUESTIONS

Make an outline for each question, listing the major points you want to discuss. Then write your practice essay, following your outline carefully and making sure that you do not skip any of your major points. At this time, you will want to add the relevant dates and details that will make your essay persuasive and accurate.

## Change Over Time

There really aren't any Change Over Time questions relevant yet. There needs to be more *time* for change to happen. This will be an important part of later chapters, but it's still too premature.

## Compare and Contrast

1. Which was more significant means of cultural and technological development, diffusion or independent invention? Give at least three examples to support your conclusion.
2. How did Phoenicia differ from the civilizations of Egypt, Assyria, and Israel?

## General Essay

1. What are the causes, means, and consequences of large-scale migrations of people? Use examples from at least three peoples.
2. Why is the Assyrian Empire considered to be the first in the world? What were its attributes and legacies?
3. Discuss the use of the Bible as a historical source. What are the advantages and disadvantages of such use for the scholar? Compare and contrast some of the biblical interpretations with those suggested by some modern historians.

# COMPARISON CHARTS

Using information gathered from the text, fill in the blank areas of each chart with the relevant data pertaining to the regions and categories listed. (Not all blank areas will necessarily be equally complete.)

Chart 3.1

## MIGRATIONS

| | When | Original Homeland | Destination | Why | Livelihood | Method of Migration | Response of Native Peoples |
|---|---|---|---|---|---|---|---|
| **Assyrians** | | | | | | | |
| **Israelites** | | | | | | | |
| **Phoenicians** | | | | | | | |

Chart 3.2

## TWO EMPIRES

| | Regions | Government System | Military Technology | Nonmilitary Technology | Economy | Society | Status of Women | Role of Civilians |
|---|---|---|---|---|---|---|---|---|
| **Assyria** | | | | | | | | |
| **Phoenicia** | | | | | | | | |

## DIVERSITY AND DOMINANCE

After reading "Diversity and Dominance: An Israeli Prophet Chastizes the Ruling Class" in your text, answer the following additional questions.

1. What must it have been like to live in the Samaria of Amos's time?
2. Do you think the poor would have supported him or the government and the Jewish Temple?

## INTERNET ASSIGNMENT

**Keywords:** **Mask of Agamemnon** or **Mycenaean mask**

**Solomon's Temple**

The Mask of Agamemnon and Solomon's Temple are both symbols of their cultures. Use the above keywords to find websites about these artifacts. You might want to consult the *History WIRED* image library on the Bulliet, *The Earth and Its Peoples* website (refer to the preface of this study guide for information on how to locate the Bulliet home page).

1. Why do you think these artifacts are seen as symbols of their cultures?
2. When was the Mycenaean Mask discovered and under what circumstances? How did that effect how we view Greek history today?
3. How can Solomon's Temple be a symbol of Jewish history and culture when it no longer stands?

## INTERNET EXPLORATION

Underwater archaeology is a growing, exciting field, and new discoveries are made each year. Recently archaeologists have found a number of sunken Phoenician ships. This is particularly helpful because we know little about the Phoenicians. Use the keywords "Phoenician shipwrecks" to learn more about what the Phoenicians shipped and about the controversy surrounding their identity.

## MAP EXERCISES

On Outline Map 3.1, shade in these areas:

Assyrian Empire

Phoenicia

Israel

Judah

Egypt

Then plot Babylon, Galilee, and Canaan.

On Outline Map 3.2, shade in:

Crete and the extent of the Minoan civilization

The extent of the Mycenaean civilization

## Outline Map 3.1

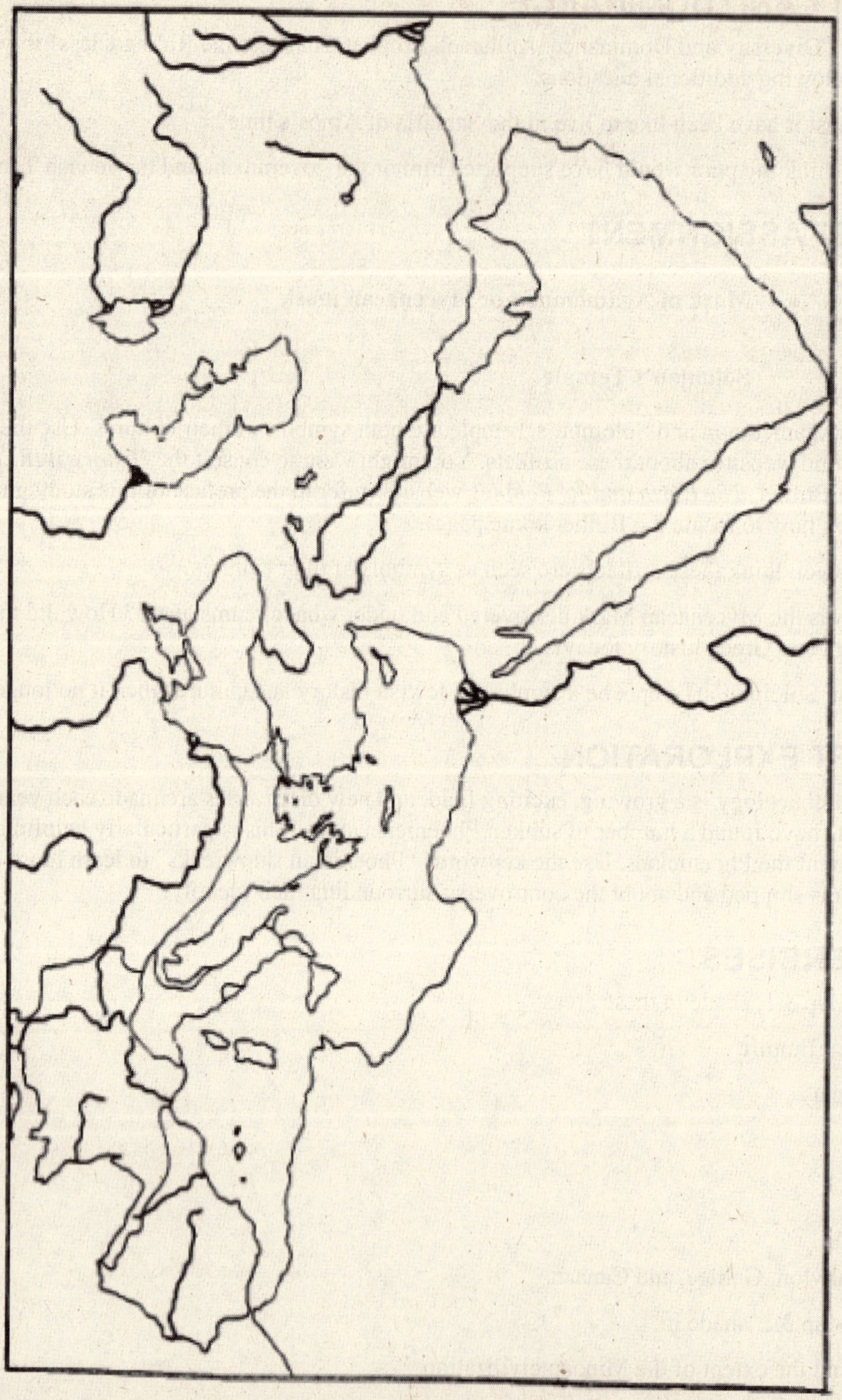

## Outline Map 3.2

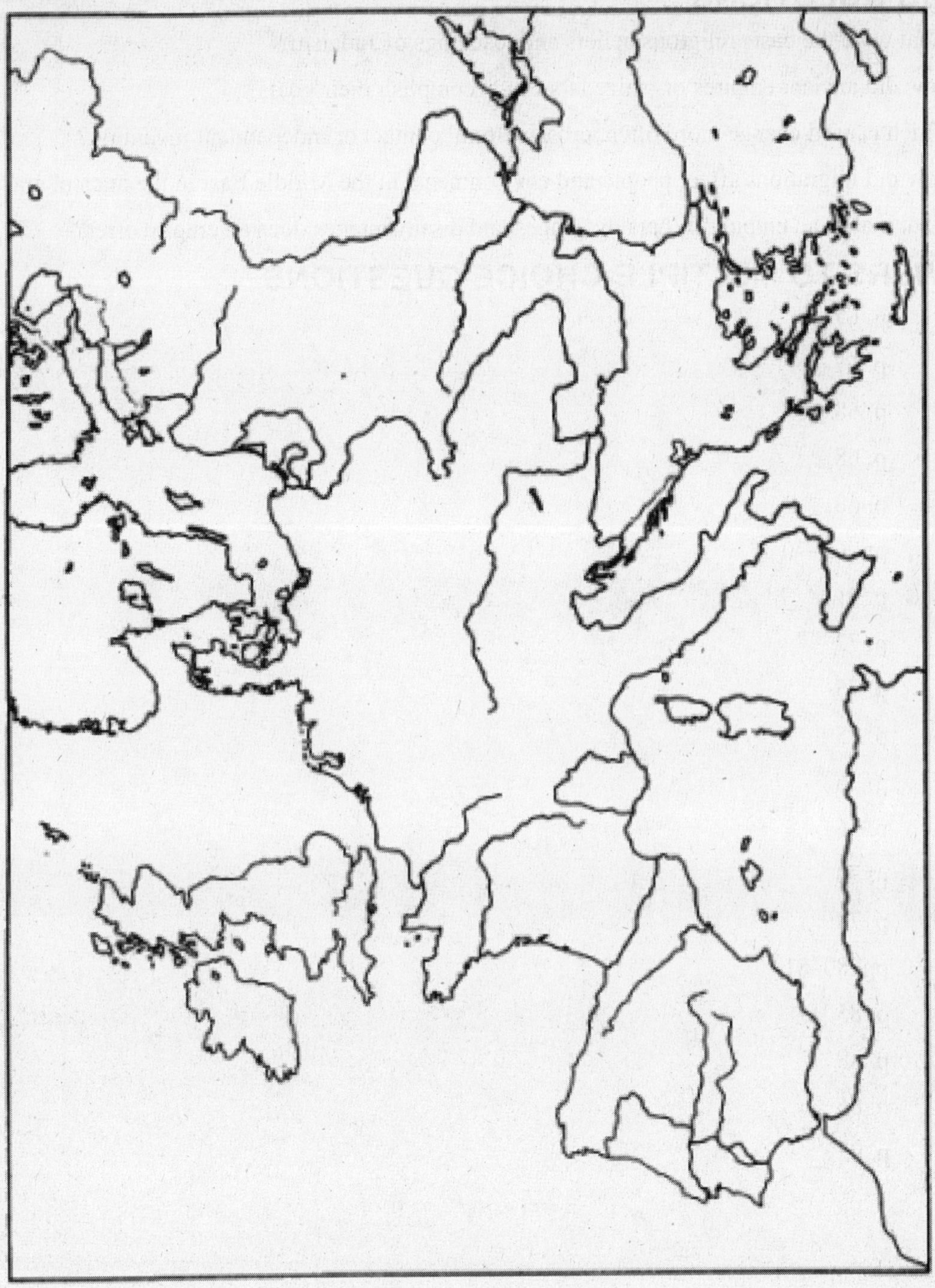

## FOCUS QUESTIONS

1. What were the basic religious beliefs and teachings of Judaism?
2. How did ancient empires organize labor to accomplish their goals?
3. Which caused change more often, cross-cultural contact or independent invention?
4. How did migrations affect people and environments in the Middle East in the ancient era?
5. What makes an empire? What advantages and disadvantages does an empire offer?

## ANSWERS TO MULTIPLE-CHOICE QUESTIONS

1. d p. 67
2. e p. 67
3. d p. 68
4. a p. 68
5. c p. 68
6. b pp. 69–70
7. b p. 71
8. a p. 72
9. a p. 75
10. c p. 75
11. a p. 76
12. b p. 76
13. a p. 78
14. a p. 79
15. a pp. 80–81
16. c p. 85
17. b p. 88
18. b p. 86
19. c p. 92

CHAPTER 4

# Greece and Iran, 1000–30 B.C.E.

## BEFORE YOU BEGIN

Chapters 4–6 examine civilizations in Africa and Eurasia during the Classical Era. Chapter 7 then deals with the more general trends that transcend any one specific place or civilization in the Foundations time period. As you read, ask yourself what subtle differences you notice between the Classical civilizations in Chapters 4–6 and the Ancient civilizations in Chapters 1–3.

## LEARNING OBJECTIVES

After reading Chapter 4 and completing this study chapter, you should be able to:

- Explain how trade networks in Eurasia functioned as links between western Asia and southern and Central Asia, and how their history has been influenced by this role.
- Explain how Persia rose from nomadic roots to become the largest land empire the world had ever seen, both with original innovations and borrowed culture from its Mesopotamian predecessors.
- Discuss the ways in which the civilizations of the Mediterranean region offered both opportunities and limited choices for its inhabitants based on social class or gender.
- Describe how Greek civilization developed and evolved into a sophisticated culture, often marred by competition among the various Greek city-states.
- Explain what characterized the relationship between the Persians and the Greeks, and how much they had in common despite being rivals.

## IDENTIFICATIONS

Define each term and explain why it is significant, including any important dates.

**Cyrus (Kurush)**

______________________________________________

______________________________________________

**Darius I (Darayavaush)**

______________________________________________

______________________________________________

**satrap**

______________________________________________

______________________________________________

**Persepolis (Parsa)**

**Zoroastrianism**

**polis**

**Athens**

**Sparta**

**tyrant**

**democracy**

**humanism**

**Herodotus**

**anthropomorphic**

**Pericles**

**Persian Wars**

**trireme**

**Socrates**

**Plato**

**Aristotle**

**Peloponnesian War**

**Alexander**

**Hellenistic Age**

**Ptolemies**

**Alexandria**

## MULTIPLE-CHOICE QUESTIONS

Read the entire question, including *all* the possible answers. Then choose the *one* answer that best fits the question.

1. The geographic location of Iran (ancient Persia)
   a. makes it a formidable barrier between east and west.
   b. makes it a link among West, South, and Central Asia.
   c. indicates that the major trading routes, such as the Silk Road, did not pass through it.
   d. indicates that the region received plenty of monsoonal rainfall, eliminating the need for large-scale irrigation.
   e. provided many fine natural harbors.
2. Which of the following statements best characterizes the differences between the Medes and the Persians?
   a. They formed two distinct ethnic groups, speaking mutually unintelligible dialects.
   b. There was no difference between them because both names refer to the same people.
   c. They were often at odds with each other throughout Iran's history.
   d. They were so similar that the Greeks could not tell them apart.
   e. Only the Medes were Indo-Europeans.
3. Which of the following best describes the general nature of Greek gods?

   I. The gods were immortal but imperfect, having many human personality faults

   II. The gods were extremely powerful and could use their power over humans for good or evil.

   III. The gods were largely uninterested in the details of human affairs and cared only that humans show them proper respect and veneration.

   IV. The gods were former humans who had been elevated to divine status by great acts of courage or heroism.

   a. I and II only
   b. I and III only
   c. I, II, and IV only
   d. II and IV only
   e. II, III, and IV only
4. Why did satrapies have more autonomy the farther they were from the central seat of government?
   a. Communication was so slow that it was impractical to refer matters to the central government.
   b. Outlying areas were constantly beguiled by neighboring peoples to follow their own course.
   c. Outlying areas were too hard to defend from invasions, so the central government did not care to monitor them closely.
   d. The Persian king always put his biggest rivals at the periphery of his kingdom and gave them more autonomy to prevent rebellion.
   e. Outlying areas were less fertile and less profitable and therefore of less interest to the government.
5. What did the walled garden called paradayadam (paradise) symbolize to the Persians?
   a. Heaven
   b. The divinity of the king
   c. The superiority of the leisure class
   d. The biblical garden of Eden
   e. The prosperity that the king and empire brought to loyal followers

6. Which group of Persian workers received the most pay?
   a. All were paid equally.
   b. Men
   c. Women
   d. Children
   e. Pregnant women
7. For the Greeks and other peoples living around it, the Mediterranean was
   a. a barrier to trade.
   b. a barrier to invasion.
   c. somewhat of a barrier to trade and invasion.
   d. a highway to the lands surrounding it.
   e. irrelevant to their affairs.
8. Which of the following did *not* help inaugurate the outward-looking seafaring activities of the Greek Archaic period?
   a. Scarcity of resources
   b. The competition between Athens and Sparta
   c. The difficulty of overland trade
   d. The availability of good anchorages
   e. Few mineral deposits
9. When the Greeks developed their alphabet, it
   a. was probably used for economic purposes, such as keeping inventories.
   b. may have been originally used to write theatrical plays.
   c. brought about immediate literacy to Greek society.
   d. was so difficult to use that only scribes could learn it.
   e. was used only to write poetry.
10. Which of the following about Greek colonies is *not* true?
    a. The colonists set out after receiving a blessing from the goddess Athena.
    b. Some colonists did not go willingly.
    c. Colonies provided a population safety valve.
    d. Colonists often reduced the native populations of their new colonies to a servile status.
    e. Moving was seen as a way to escape poverty.
11. What was the central ritual of Greek religion?
    a. Baptism
    b. Sacrifice
    c. Fasting
    d. Feasting
    e. The predictions of oracles
12. Why is Herodotus considered the father of history?
    a. He wrote many narratives of Greek events.
    b. He was the first person to record history.
    c. He was the first Greek to get paid to teach history.
    d. He sought the causes behind historical events.
    e. He was a logographer.
13. What enabled the rowers of Athenian battleships to gain an equal voice in the democratic system?
    a. The Hoplite Revolt
    b. The war with the Minoans
    c. A vote in the Athenian Assembly
    d. The great importance of the navy to the Athenian military
    e. The Delian League's adoption of democracy

14. What motivated the theft of Alexander the Great's corpse by members of the Ptolemaic dynasty?
    a. They wanted to denigrate and humiliate the former Greek empire of Alexander.
    b. The theft was an attempt to gain legitimacy for Ptolemaic rule by claiming Alexander's blessing.
    c. They believed it would prove to their rivals that they had the military capability to carry out such a great scheme.
    d. They believed his corpse would bring them good fortune.
    e. They feared Alexander's ghost and sought to contain it.
15. To the Persians, the conflict with the Greeks
    a. was all-consuming.
    b. was very important to the survival of their kingdom.
    c. was less important than it was to the Greeks.
    d. seemed inconsequential.
    e. was more important than their conflicts with Central Asians.

## ESSAY QUESTIONS

Make an outline for each question, listing the major points you want to discuss. Then write your practice essay, following your outline carefully and making sure that you do not skip any of your major points. At this time, you will want to add the relevant dates and details that will make your essay persuasive and accurate.

### Change Over Time

1. Discuss the legacy of Greece and Persia. What effect did they have on their neighbors and on their descendants?

### Compare and Contrast

1. Compare and contrast the Greek and Persian civilizations. What cultural traits, religious beliefs, and social organizations separated them? Which of these attributes did they share?
2. Compare the division of labor among social classes and genders in Greece and Persia.
3. Compare and contrast Sparta and Athens. What differences and similarities can be seen in their histories, government systems, goals, and societies? How did they interact?

### General Essay

1. Discuss the effect of the physical environment on Persia and Greece. What aspects of the geography and climate influenced the development of their societies?

## COMPARISON CHARTS

Using information gathered from the text, fill in the blank areas of each chart with the relevant data pertaining to the regions and categories listed. (Not all blank areas will necessarily be equally complete.)

Chart 4.1

**TWO APPROACHES TO RELIGION**

| | God(s) | Cosmology | Basic Tenets | Morality/ Sin | Practices | Role of Humans | Outside Influences | Older Traditions | Government Use |
|---|---|---|---|---|---|---|---|---|---|
| **Persia: Zoroastrianism** | | | | | | | | | |
| **Greece** | | | | | | | | | |

Chart 4.2

## PHASES OF GREEK HISTORY

| | Dates | Defining Event | Population | Government System | Dominant Region | Society | Trade/ Economics | Technology | Religion | Foreign Affairs | Migration |
|---|---|---|---|---|---|---|---|---|---|---|---|
| Minoans | | | | | | | | | | | |
| Mycenae | | | | | | | | | | | |
| Dark Ages | | | | | | | | | | | |
| Archaic Greece | | | | | | | | | | | |
| Classical Greece | | | | | | | | | | | |
| Hellenistic Age | | | | | | | | | | | |

## DIVERSITY AND DOMINANCE

After reading "Diversity and Dominance: The Persian View of Kingship" in your text, answer the following additional questions.

1. By what means does Darius claim to have attained power? Why does he provide such a long list of victorious battles?
2. Do you see the parallel that Darius draws between Ahuramazda and himself, and then between his rule and his subject peoples?

## INTERNET ASSIGNMENT

**Keywords:** **Acropolis of Athens**

**the Gate of All Nations** or **Takt-e-Jamshid**

Both the Acropolis of Athens and the city of Persepolis, where the Gate of All Nations is located, were ceremonial centers. Use the above keywords to find websites about these topics. You might want to consult the *History WIRED* image library on the Bulliet, *The Earth and Its Peoples* website (refer to the preface of this study guide for information on how to locate the Bulliet home page).

1. How did the two monuments differ in size and location?
2. How did they differ in style and building materials?
3. What can account for these differences?

## INTERNET EXPLORATION

Theories abound about Atlantis, and hardly a month goes by without another television special on the subject. How sound are these theories? Use the keywords "lost continent of Atlantis" to see some of the better and some of the more imaginative theories. Evaluate the scientific and historical evidence that is used to back up those theories. Why were the ancient Greeks so fascinated with the possibility of a lost continent? Why are we?

## MAP EXERCISES

On Outline Map 4.1, shade in these areas:

Greek colonization

Phoenician colonization

Peloponnese

Lydia

Anatolia

Ionia

Then plot the following:

Carthage

Corinth

Crete

Phoenicia

Mediterranean Sea

On Outline Map 4.2, shade in the Persian homeland and outline the growth of the Persian Empire to its greatest extent. Then plot the following:

Susa

Persepolis

Royal Road

Lydia

## Outline Map 4.1

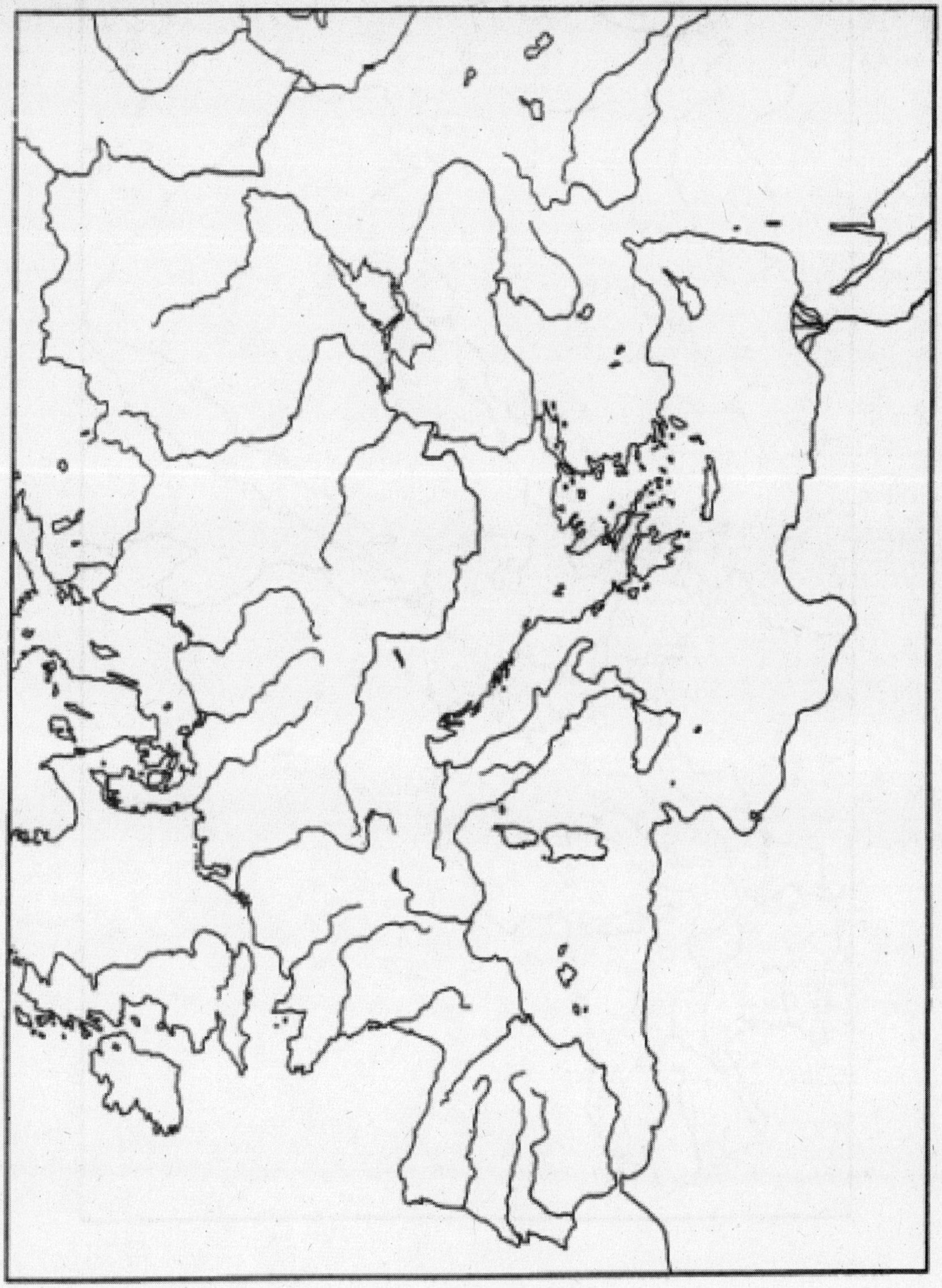

## Outline Map 4.2

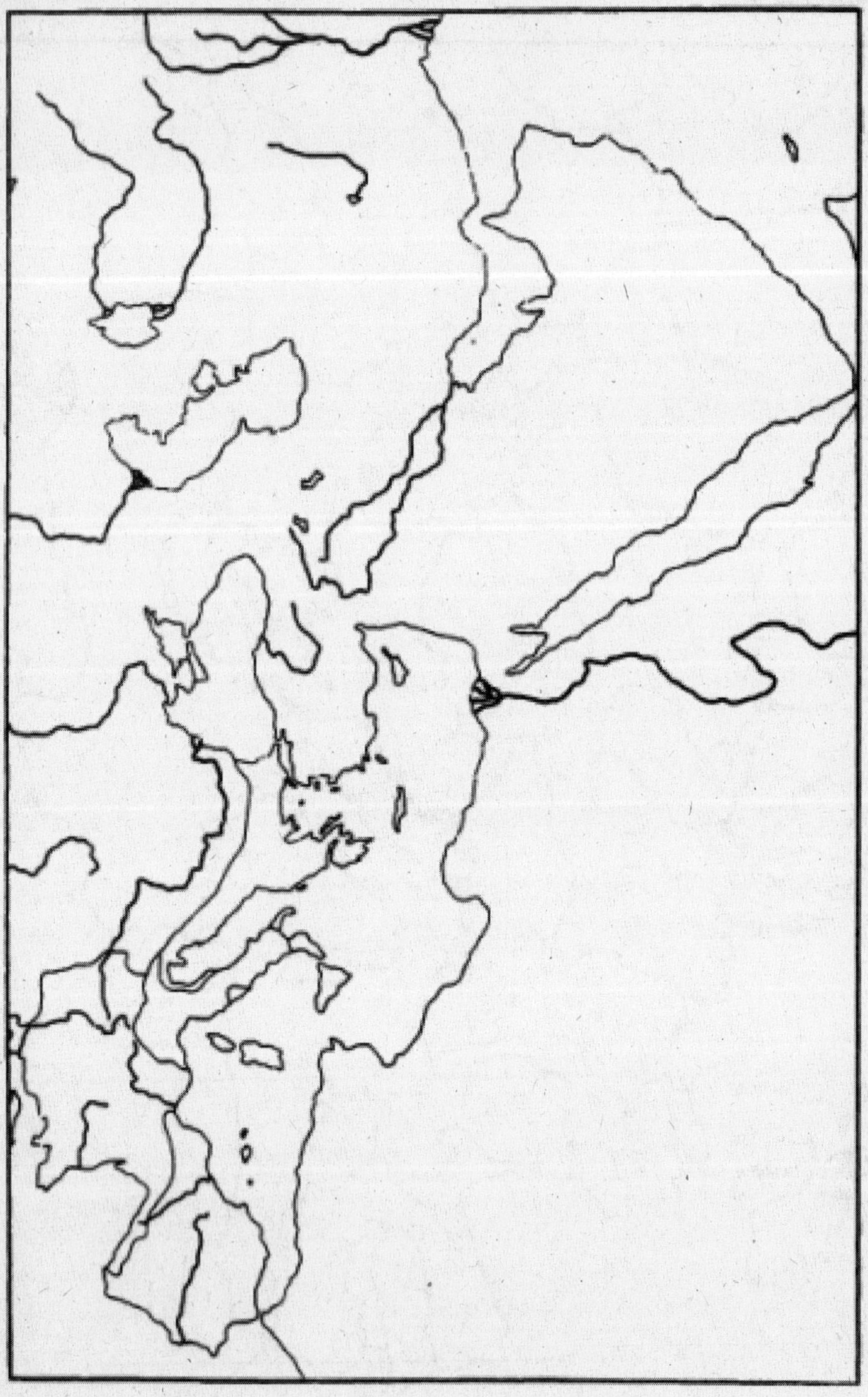

## FOCUS QUESTIONS

1. How did trade networks in Eurasia function as a link between western Asia and southern and Central Asia?
2. How did Persia rise from nomadic roots to become the largest land empire the world had ever seen?
3. How did the civilizations of the Mediterranean region offer both opportunities and limited choices for its inhabitants based on social class or gender?
4. How did Greek civilization develop and evolve into a sophisticated culture, in spite of competition among the various Greek city-states?
5. Did the Persians and the Greeks share more in common with each other or were they fundamentally different?

## ANSWERS TO MULTIPLE-CHOICE QUESTIONS

1. b p. 100
2. d p. 103
3. a p. 114
4. a p. 104
5. e p. 105
6. e p. 105
7. d p. 111
8. b p. 111
9. a p. 111
10. a p. 112
11. b p. 114
12. d p. 116
13. d p. 119
14. b p. 127
15. c p. 117

CHAPTER 5

# An Age of Empires: Rome and Han China, 753 B.C.E.–600 C.E.

## BEFORE YOU BEGIN

This chapter encourages direct comparisons between two Classical empires. As you read about Rome and Han China, constantly ask yourself how the political, economic, religious, social, and technological characteristics of each empire compare. Good students will be able to categorize famous examples of similarities and differences into "political" or "religious" labels, but superior students will find similarities *within* differences, and differences *within* similarities. This kind of sophisticated analysis is a major goal of AP World History.

## LEARNING OBJECTIVES

After reading Chapter 5 and completing this study chapter, you should be able to:

- Explain and compare the political, social, economic, and technological characteristics of two great empires at opposite ends of the Eurasian continent.
- Explain how the Silk Road promoted the trade of goods and ideas between the two empires through intermediaries, but it never *directly* linked their peoples.
- Explain how religion and/or philosophy in Rome and China helped define their respective cultures and shape the destinies of these empires.
- Explain and compare the factors that may have contributed to the fall of Rome and Han China, and explain the factors that may have allowed China to continue as a cohesive cultural system, while Rome eventually evolved into a collection of discrete states.

## IDENTIFICATIONS

Define each term and explain why it is significant, including any important dates.

**Roman Republic**

______________________________________________

______________________________________________

**Roman Senate**

______________________________________________

______________________________________________

**patron/client relationship**

______________________________________________

______________________________________________

**Roman Principate**

**Augustus**

***equites***

***pax romana***

**Romanization**

**Jesus**

**Paul**

**roads**

**aqueduct**

**concrete**

**third-century crisis**

**Diocletian**

**Constantine**

**Constantinople**

**Qin**

**Shi Huangdi**

**census**

**Han**

**Chang'an**

**gentry**

**Xiongnu**

**Kongzi/Confucius**

## MULTIPLE-CHOICE QUESTIONS

Read the entire question, including *all* the possible answers. Then choose the *one* answer that best fits the question.

1. In agricultural societies, the basis of wealth is
   a. the peasants.
   b. the land.
   c. food.
   d. trade.
   e. precious metals.
2. During the Roman Republic, all adult male citizens had the right to vote
   a. and so Rome was a democracy.
   b. and so there was equal representation.
   c. and so everyone was equally powerless.
   d. but the votes were weighted so that the votes of the wealthy counted for more.
   e. but the votes of poor men were not counted.
3. The term for Roman senators was
   a. one year.
   b. four years.
   c. ten years.
   d. twenty-five years.
   e. life.
4. In a legal sense, Roman women
   a. never ceased being children.
   b. were nearly equal to men.
   c. were completely equal to men.
   d. were equal only to poor men.
   e. were superior to men.
5. Which of the following provides the most convincing explanation for Rome's expansion?
   a. The Romans were greedy and aggressive.
   b. The Roman Consuls wanted military glory.
   c. The Romans were only defending themselves.
   d. The Romans feared an attack and so wanted a buffer zone.
   e. The Romans loved the thrill of battle.
6. Why did people during the time of the Roman Republic become dependent on expensive, imported grain?
   a. There was a large population explosion in the second century B.C.E.
   b. The grain was of higher quality than domestic grain.
   c. Roman religion forbade agriculture.
   d. Large landowners preferred to graze cattle or grow cash crops.
   e. This dependence was necessary in order to import silk from China.
7. The missionary career of the Apostle Paul
   a. was mostly unsuccessful.
   b. exemplifies the cosmopolitan nature of the Roman Empire.
   c. ended in imprisonment in India.
   d. was narrow because he limited his message to Jews only.
   e. was inhibited by the *pax romana*.

8. Aqueducts worked with the aid of
   a. human muscle power.
   b. donkeys.
   c. gravity.
   d. solar-powered pumps.
   e. water wheels.
9. Why did the people of the Late Roman Empire revert to a barter economy?
   a. The kingdoms they were trading with did not use money.
   b. None of Rome's trading partners would accept Roman currency because they did not trust the Roman banking system.
   c. The emperors were cutting back on the precious metals in the coins, thereby causing them to be devalued.
   d. It was more efficient for an illiterate people.
   e. Rome never reverted to a barter economy.
10. Which of the following is *not* one of the reasons that Constantine moved the capital of the Roman Empire to Constantinople?
    a. The eastern Roman Empire was more threatened by the possibility of invasion.
    b. The middle class of the eastern Roman Empire was wealthier.
    c. There were more Christians in the east.
    d. There were few Christians in the eastern Roman Empire, so there was more opportunity to gain new converts.
    e. There were more educated people in the eastern Roman Empire.
11. Why did the majority of the Chinese population during the Han dynasty live in eastern China?
    a. They wanted access to sea trade and its accompanying wealth.
    b. The best farmland was concentrated in eastern China.
    c. They were more isolated from invasion from nomadic peoples there.
    d. The best Buddhist centers were in eastern China.
    e. This was the extent of the Chinese empire.
12. The Qin government abolished slavery because
    a. it thought that making people work for the state for free was immoral.
    b. slavery was against the tenets of Confucianism.
    c. slavery was against the tenets of Buddhism.
    d. slaves did not pay taxes, but free people did.
    e. it was forced to do so by the great slave revolt of 208 B.C.E.
13. Roads were originally built in Rome and China to
    a. facilitate trade.
    b. move troops.
    c. confuse enemies.
    d. enable the construction of massive monuments.
    e. encourage migration.
14. When the Han took over, they
    a. completely reinstated the Zhou system.
    b. completely eradicated all remnants of Qin rule.
    c. retained the Qin system with minor modifications.
    d. got rid of everything but Legalism.
    e. retained the entire Qin system without change.

15. China's most valuable commodity was
    a. silk.
    b. tea.
    c. porcelain.
    d. opium.
    e. salt.
16. Which of the following does *not* represent one way in which the Chinese tried to control nomadic raids?
    a. They paid protection money.
    b. They placed friendly people around the border as a buffer.
    c. They tried to reason with the nomads, citing the Buddhist principle of nonviolence.
    d. They tried to beat the nomads in outright warfare.
    e. They gave them Chinese princesses as brides.
17. Which of the following best describes the degree of contact between the Roman and Han Empires?
    a. Roman and Han Chinese armies conquered the intermediary empires and peoples, forming a direct border northwest of the Hindu Kush in Persia (modern-day Iran).
    b. Christian missionaries evangelized small numbers of Chinese peasants, using the silk roads as a transportation system.
    c. Chinese naval forces brought ambassadors of the Han emperor to the Red Sea, where diplomatic contact was made with Roman provincial governors.
    d. Roman and Han Chinese citizens never met each other directly, but there was an indirect economic connection via the silk roads.
    e. Advisers to both the Roman and Han Chinese emperors persuaded the emperors not to pursue any contact with the other.
18. All of the following were reasons that centralized political rule reemerged in China but not in Europe after this period *except*:
    a. Chinese society had a more deeply ingrained political tradition of seeing individuals as subservient to the state than did the Roman Empire.
    b. unlike Han China, the Roman Empire had more opportunities for social and economic mobility, which encouraged individual rejection of centralized governmental authority.
    c. despite claims of divine status, the Roman emperor was never venerated to the degree that the Chinese viewed their emperor per the Mandate of Heaven.
    d. Christianity weakened the Roman emperor's claim to divinity, while Buddhism was more easily reconciled with Chinese Confucian traditions.
    e. the geography of the Mediterranean Sea encouraged political fragmentation, while the Great Wall of China symbolized the necessity of a single emperor to coordinate defense from attacks by nomadic peoples.

## ESSAY QUESTIONS

Make an outline for each question, listing the major points you want to discuss. Then write your practice essay, following your outline carefully and making sure that you do not skip any of your major points. At this time, you will want to add the relevant dates and details that will make your essay persuasive and accurate.

## Change Over Time

1. Trace the rise of the Chinese empire from the Qin state through the end of the Han dynasty. What factors were influential in its rise and fall? Account for the continuity of the Chinese culture in the face of war and dynastic change. Why did this continuity not exist to such a great extent in Rome?
2. How did the Silk Road promote the trade of goods and ideas between the two empires? Be careful to accurately describe the *degree* of contact (or *lack* of contact) between the two empires.
3. How did religion and/or philosophy in Rome and China help people define their respective cultures and shape the destinies of these empires?

## Compare and Contrast

1. Compare and contrast the empires of Rome and Han China. How were they structured? What methods did they use to keep order and gain prosperity? How successful were they? What weaknesses eventually led to their downfall?
2. Discuss the importance of trade to Rome and China. Who were their trading partners, and what was traded? How vital was trade to the economy of each empire? How did each empire view trade?
3. Compare and contrast the three major philosophies of early China: Confucianism, Legalism, and Daoism. What views did they offer on the relationship between the people and the state? How did they claim to be able to control the populace? How did each propose to solve the problems of the time? What was their success rate?
4. Compare and contrast the role of the individual in Rome and Han China. How did the individual function in the family? How did the view of the individual affect society?
5. Compare the characteristics of Han China and Rome in any *three* of the following categories.
   a. Political structure
   b. Social mobility
   c. Economic basis
   d. Technological accomplishments
6. How were the effects of the fall of the Roman Empire different from the fall of Han China? Why did these differences occur?

## COMPARISON CHARTS

Using information gathered from the text, fill in the blank areas of each chart with the relevant data pertaining to the regions and categories listed. (Not all blank areas will necessarily be equally complete.)

Chart 5.1

ROME

| | Roman Republic | Roman Empire |
|---|---|---|
| Dates | | |
| Political Systems | | |
| Sources of Elite Power | | |
| Notable Rulers | | |
| Slavery | | |
| Social Structure | | |
| Family Structure | | |
| Religion | | |
| Trade and Economics | | |
| Laws | | |
| Technology | | |
| Citizenship | | |
| Housing | | |
| Women | | |
| External Relations | | |
| Expansion | | |
| Internal Relations | | |
| Demise | | |
| Successful States | | |

Chart 5.2

HAN CHINA

| | Qin Empire | Earlier Han | Later Han |
|---|---|---|---|
| Dates | | | |
| Political Systems | | | |
| Sources of Government Power | | | |
| Notable Rulers | | | |
| Slavery | | | |
| Social Structure | | | |
| Family Structure | | | |
| Religion/Philosophy | | | |
| Trade and Economics | | | |
| Laws | | | |
| Technology | | | |
| Women | | | |
| Internal Relations | | | |
| External Relations | | | |
| Expansion | | | |
| Successful States | | | |

## DIVERSITY AND DOMINANCE

After reading "Diversity and Dominance: The Treatment of Slaves in Rome and China" in your text, answer the following additional questions.

1. How were slaves procured in Rome and China?
2. What kinds of tasks were slaves generally required to perform?
3. Were slaves as essential in China as in Rome?
4. Considering the factors mentioned in questions 1, 2, and 3, analyze the relative position that slaves had in each society.

## INTERNET ASSIGNMENT

**Keywords:** **Roman Coliseum**

**the Great Wall of China**

Monumental architecture is an important component of civilization and can serve many purposes. Use the above keywords to find websites about the Roman Coliseum and the Great Wall. You might want to consult the *History WIRED* image library on the Bulliet, *The Earth and Its Peoples* website (refer to the preface of this study guide for information on how to locate the Bulliet home page).

1. What purpose did the Roman Coliseum and the Great Wall serve in Rome and China?
2. What kind of human power would it take to build such structures, and how might that power have been compelled and organized?
3. How can these two structures be symbols of both identity and cruelty?

## INTERNET EXPLORATION

Ever wondered what it felt like to stand in the center of the Coliseum, facing a daunting enemy, with the roar of the crowd surrounding you? Use the keywords "Roman gladiators" to look at some websites on this Roman figure. You will also find sites on the recent movie *Gladiator*. What makes a society interested in these kinds of very dangerous games? Why were the Romans fascinated with fighting to the death? Why are Americans today fascinated with feats of strength and skills necessary to be good fighters?

## MAP EXERCISES

On Outline Map 5.1, shade in the Roman Empire at its greatest extent and also the Parthian Empire. Then plot Rome.

On Outline Map 5.2, shade in the area ruled by the Han dynasty and outline the area ruled by the Qin dynasty. Then plot the following:

Chang'an

Silk Road

Great Wall

Monsoon winds

## Outline Map 5.1

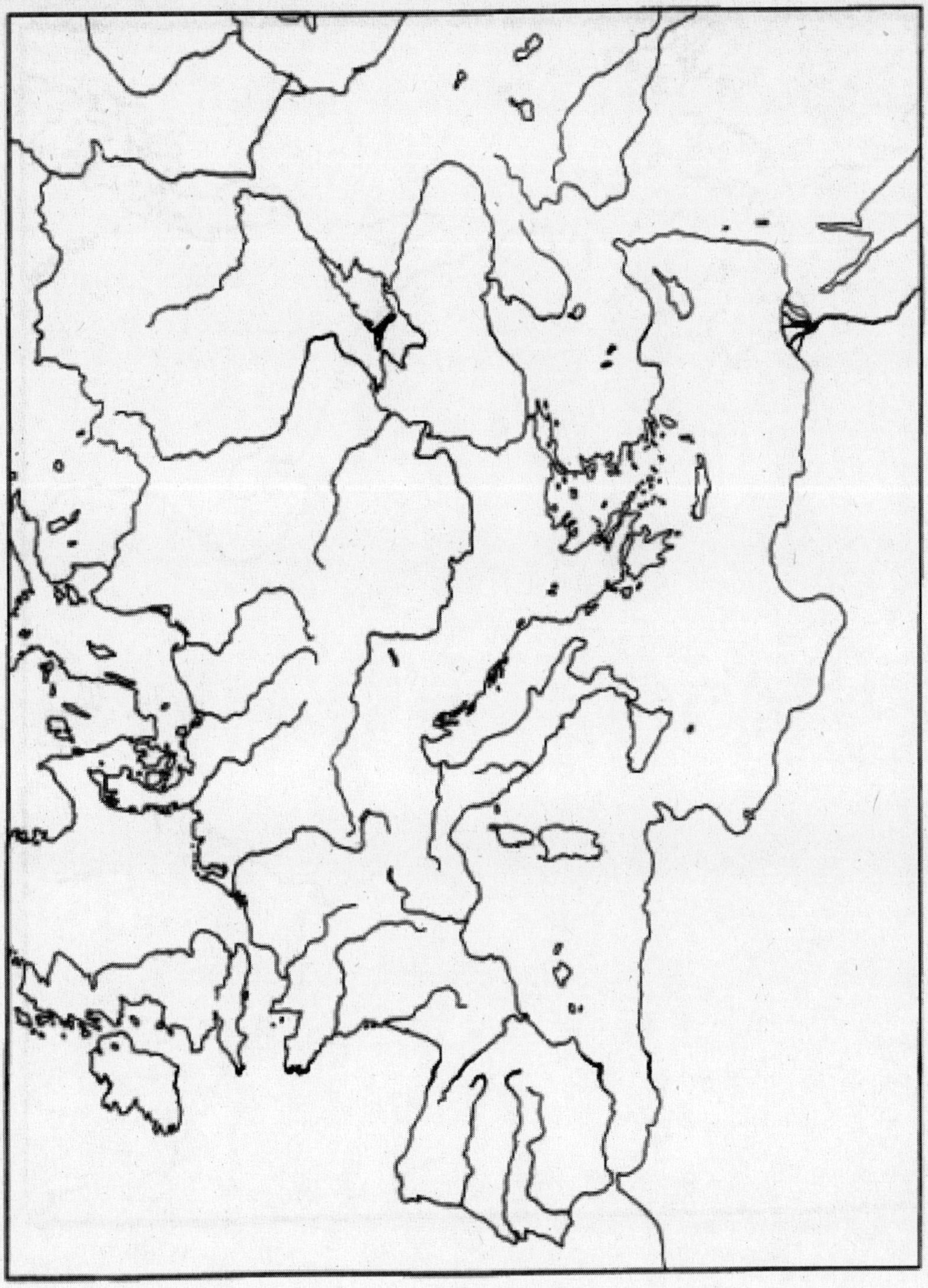

## Outline Map 5.2

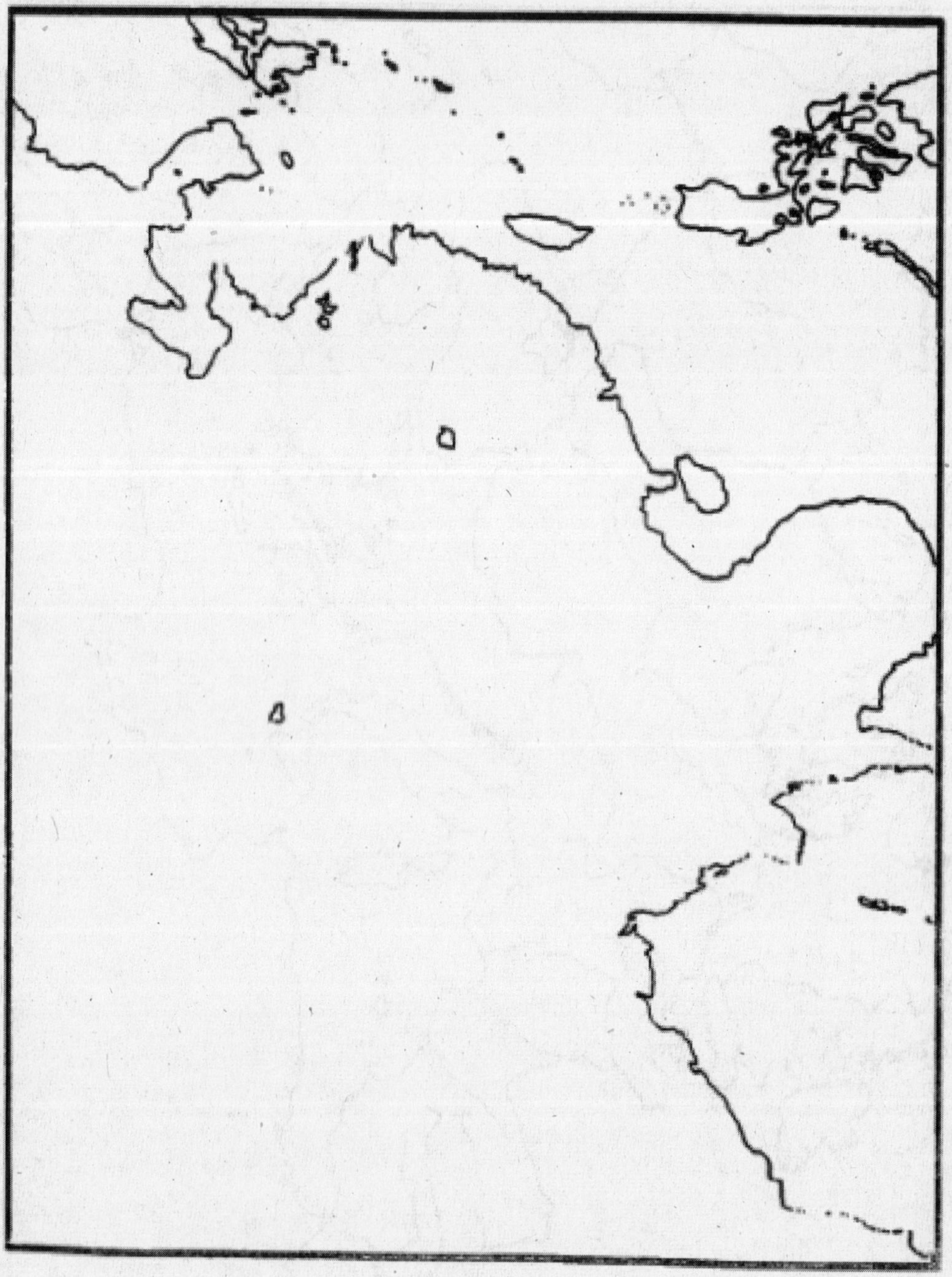

## FOCUS QUESTIONS

1. How do the political, social, economic, and technological characteristics of Han China and Rome compare?
2. How did the Silk Road promote the trade of goods and ideas between Han China and Rome? Be careful to accurately describe the *degree* of contact (or *lack* of contact) between the two empires.
3. How did religion and/or philosophy in Rome and China help people define their respective cultures and shape the destinies of these empires?
4. How were the effects of the fall of the Roman Empire different from the fall of Han China? Why did these differences occur?

## ANSWERS TO MULTIPLE-CHOICE QUESTIONS

1. b p. 136
2. d p. 139
3. e p. 139
4. a pp. 139–140
5. d p. 140
6. d p. 141
7. b p. 147
8. c p. 147
9. c p. 149
10. d p. 150
11. b p. 153
12. d p. 155
13. b p. 155
14. c p. 155
15. a p. 158
16. c p. 158
17. d p. 136
18. e pp. 159–160

CHAPTER 6

# India and Southeast Asia, 1500 B.C.E.–600 C.E.

## BEFORE YOU BEGIN

The biggest challenge about this chapter is that most students in the United States have very little familiarity with the history of the Indian subcontinent. The vocabulary of the empires, people, and rulers can seem overwhelming at first. Avoid the tendency to unnecessarily and inaccurately treat this chapter's content as exotic and "other," while seeing previous chapters' cultures as "normal." As you become more familiar with this part of the world, you'll soon recognize many of the same patterns of political, religious, economic, and technological development that you've studied in previous chapters.

## LEARNING OBJECTIVES

After reading Chapter 6 and completing this study chapter, you should be able to:

- Explain how the environments of India and Southeast Asia influenced the choice of the livelihood of the people, as well as the development of distinct social and governmental structures.
- Explain how India evolved a complex social system and distinct religious systems to meet the needs of its society.
- Explain how the region of Southeast Asia developed into a major trading center and how sophisticated government systems and social structures arose both from native traditions and as a result of outside influence from India and China.
- Discuss the Indian scientific and technological advancements that developed between 1500 B.C.E. and 600 C.E. and indicate which of them still influence us today.
- Discuss the major beliefs of Hinduism and Buddhism and how they agree or disagree.
- Discuss the major political developments in India and Southeast Asia up to the year 600 C.E., especially the Mauryan and Gupta Empires.

## IDENTIFICATIONS

Define each term and explain why it is significant, including any important dates.

**subcontinent**

______________________________________________

______________________________________________

**monsoon**

______________________________________________

______________________________________________

**Vedas**

**varna**

**jati**

**karma**

**moksha**

**Buddha**

**Mahayana Buddhism**

**Theravada Buddhism**

**atman**

**reincarnation**

**Hinduism**

**Mauryan Empire**

**Ashoka**

**Mahabharata**

**Bhagavad-Gita**

**nirvana**

**bhakti**

**Vishnu**

**Tamil kingdoms**

**Gupta Empire**

**theater-state**

**Malay peoples**

**puja**

**water resource "boards"**

**Funan**

**Srivijaya**

**Borobodur**

**"Arabic" numerals**

## MULTIPLE-CHOICE QUESTIONS

Read the entire question, including *all* the possible answers. Then choose the *one* answer that best fits the question.

1. Indo-European nomads tended to be
   a. matriarchal.
   b. patriarchal.
   c. pacifist.
   d. agricultural.
   e. insular.
2. Why did members of the higher castes fear contact with the lower castes?
   a. They feared pollution from contact with lower-caste individuals.
   b. The lower castes were believed to be a bad influence on upper-caste children.
   c. They did not want the lower castes to become Hindus.
   d. They wanted to retain Arya and Dasa blood purity.
   e. They feared leprosy.
3. Which of the following is *not* among the practices of Jainism?
   a. Strict nonviolence, emphasizing the holiness of the life force
   b. Farming in order to stay close to the land
   c. Extreme asceticism and nudity
   d. Eating so little that one starves to death
   e. Wearing masks to prevent the inhalation of small insects

4. After six years of strict asceticism, Siddhartha Gautama decided to
   a. commit suicide.
   b. enter nirvana.
   c. go home and resume his duties as a prince.
   d. adhere to a "Middle Path" of moderation.
   e. become a Jain.
5. Which of the following is *not* a characteristic of Buddhism?
   a. It denied the usefulness of gods.
   b. It viewed the individual as "soul-less."
   c. It emphasized the search for spiritual truth.
   d. It focused on living one's life in a manner that minimized desire and suffering.
   e. It demanded frequent sacrifices of small animals.
6. Why was the Buddha originally represented by symbols?
   a. Because it was more mystical
   b. So that his enemies would not recognize his temples and deface them
   c. To emphasize his achievement of a state of nonexistence
   d. Because Buddhism forbade the representation of all human forms
   e. To use his image would have made him seem less godlike
7. The incorporation of the Buddha into the Hindu pantheon
   a. was a blatant attempt to co-opt the rival religion's founder.
   b. indicated the open and all-encompassing nature of Hinduism.
   c. put an end to the rivalry between the followers of the two faiths.
   d. reflected the government's decision to patronize each religion equally.
   e. was accidental.
8. Sacrifice is the major form of worship in
   a. Brahmanism.
   b. Buddhism.
   c. Hinduism.
   d. Jainism.
   e. all Indian religions.
9. Which of the following factors did *not* contribute to a tendency toward disunity in ancient India?
   a. The different forms of organization and economic activity
   b. The threat of outside invasion
   c. The complex social hierarchy
   d. The landscape of India
   e. The differing languages and social practices
10. What purpose did Ashoka's famous stone pillars serve?
    a. They were the first line of defense in India's wars with Persia.
    b. They marked the boundaries of India.
    c. They were inscribed with his belief in nonviolence, morality, moderation, and religious tolerance both in government and in private life.
    d. They were actually burial markers.
    e. They were used to mark the rise and fall of the annual flooding of the Ganges River.
11. Why were several foreign kings in India more likely to convert to Buddhism than to Hinduism?
    a. Buddhism was a more optimistic religion.
    b. The philosophy of Buddhism is easier to understand.
    c. Hindu beliefs did not include reincarnation.
    d. Hinduism does not allow new converts.
    e. Hinduism had no easy mechanism for working foreigners into its system of class and caste.

12. The region of Southeast Asia first rose to prominence and prosperity because
    a. the two large kingdoms around it fell into ruin and decay.
    b. Europeans traded there.
    c. of its intermediary role in the trade between southern and eastern Asia.
    d. the land was unfit for agriculture, and trade was the only way to make a living.
    e. it adopted the Confucian work ethic.
13. Which of the following foodstuffs did *not* originate in Southeast Asia?
    a. Taro
    b. Chickens
    c. Bananas
    d. Sugar cane
    e. Rice
14. Which of the following was *not* among the impressive navigational skills of the inhabitants of Southeast Asia?
    a. They knew how to ride the monsoon winds.
    b. They knew how to interpret the patterns of swells.
    c. They knew how to interpret the patterns of clouds.
    d. They knew how to interpret the bird and sea life.
    e. They knew how to interpret the stars.
15. The most likely explanation for the decline of Funan in the sixth century is
    a. invasion by Chinese explorers.
    b. failure of its wet-rice crop.
    c. the marriage of its princess to an Indian Brahmin.
    d. that international trade routes changed, bypassing Funan.
    e. unknown.
16. Which of the following statements would a historian make concerning India's ethnic and political structure?
    a. India's geographic isolation caused by the Himalayas also isolated India from foreign invasions.
    b. The development of India's caste system prevented any permanent political unity because different varna were constantly fighting each other.
    c. India's ethnic identity was largely shaped by the individual rulers of the Mauryan and Gupta Empires.
    d. India possessed a wide diversity of ethnic groups, which discouraged centralized political control.
    e. Ashoka's rise to power was symbolic of the rise of the Brahmin caste and the subjugation of lower castes.
17. Which of the following best describes India's role in the global trade network prior to 600 C.E.?
    a. India was largely unimportant, operating on the periphery of most trade before 600 C.E.
    b. India was the central crossroad of trade routes linking various areas of Asia.
    c. Most trade took place north of the Himalayas, largely bypassing India.
    d. India traded extensively with China but not with Arabia.
    e. India participated in trans-regional trade extensively during the Gupta Empire but not during the earlier Mauryan Empire.

## ESSAY QUESTIONS

Make an outline for each question, listing the major points you want to discuss. Then write your practice essay, following your outline carefully and making sure that you do not skip any of your major points. At this time, you will want to add the relevant dates and details that will make your essay persuasive and accurate.

### Change Over Time

1. Analyze the role the Indian subcontinent played in the overall global trading system up to the year 600 C.E.
2. Trace the development of India from the Vedic era to the Mauryan dynasty and then to the Gupta Empire. Pay special attention to politics, religion, and social development. How did the status of women evolve in this time?
3. Discuss the origins, evolution, and basic tenets of Hinduism. How did it affect people's daily lives? What political role has it played?
4. Discuss Southeast Asian migrations. Why did people migrate? Where did they go? How did they get there? What was the impact of their migrations?
5. What two outside factors influenced the development of large states in Southeast Asia? Name those states and trace their development.

### Compare and Contrast

1. Compare the role Hinduism played in creating a social hierarchy in India to the role Confucianism played in China. How did each tradition justify one's "place" in society?
2. Compare how Hinduism and Buddhism distinguished one's role and function in society based on gender.
3. Compare the Indian caste system to other forms of social inequality (for example, slavery) studied in previous chapters.
4. Compare Jainism and Buddhism. What were their basic beliefs and practices? What were they a response to? How successful were they?

### General Essay

1. Discuss Indian diversity. What groups make up Indian society? Is this diversity a drawback or an advantage? Explain. How does it relate to the great proliferation of gods, sects, and local practices in Hinduism?

## COMPARISON CHARTS

Using information gathered from the text, fill in the blank areas of each chart with the relevant data pertaining to the regions and categories listed. (Not all blank areas will necessarily be used.)

### Chart 6.1

### WOMEN'S CHANGING ROLE IN INDIA

| | Dates | Property/ Inheritance | Marriage/ Divorce | Religion | Education | Profession | Children | Freedom of Movement |
|---|---|---|---|---|---|---|---|---|
| **Vedic Age** | | | | | | | | |
| **Mauryan Empire** | | | | | | | | |
| **Gupta Empire** | | | | | | | | |

Chart 6.2

## GROWTH OF SOUTHEAST ASIA

| | Environment | Region | Dates | Social System | Trade/ Economics | Products | Technology | Religion | Outside Influence | Language | Monumental Architecture |
|---|---|---|---|---|---|---|---|---|---|---|---|
| **Funan** | | | | | | | | | | | |
| **Srivijaya** | | | | | | | | | | | |

## DIVERSITY AND DOMINANCE

After reading "Diversity and Dominance: The Situation of Women in the *Kama Sutra*" in your text, answer the following additional questions.

1. How did marriage change society's expectation for a young woman, and how was this reflected in her behavior?
2. How many people were involved in the arrangement of a marriage?
3. How did the arrangements of a bride without parents differ from the arrangements made for a bride with living parents?
4. What do you think of some of the tactics used in marriage negotiations, and do you think they would be appropriate today?

## INTERNET ASSIGNMENT

**Keywords:** **Hindu temples**

**Borobudur**

In many societies the religious structures are the most prominent and are even the longest lasting of all the monuments created in the past. There are many fine examples of Indian Hindu temples, and many of them have a very similar shape to the Buddhist temple at Borobudur. Use the keywords above to find websites about the Indian Hindu temples and Borobudur. You might want to consult the *History WIRED* image library on the Bulliet, *The Earth and Its Peoples* website (refer to the preface of this study guide for information on how to locate the Bulliet home page).

1. What do the religious structures tend to resemble?
2. Did you find a reason for their shape?
3. Compare and contrast the Indian Hindu temples and Borobudur. What might account for any similarities and differences?

## INTERNET EXPLORATION

One of the most interesting areas of study in any society is the various gods and goddesses. Indian deities are usually thought of as anthropomorphic (humanlike). Use the keywords "Hindu gods and goddesses" to see many examples of Hindu deities. In what ways are they like humans? In what ways are they clearly not? What could account for some of the extraordinary forms that the Indian gods and goddesses take?

## MAP EXERCISES

On Outline Map 6.1, shade in the Mauryan Empire and the Gupta Empire at their greatest extent and also the Kushan Empire. Then plot the following:

Pataliputra

Ganges River

On Outline Map 6.2, shade in the Srivijayan Empire, Champa, and Annam. Then plot Srivijaya and Borobodur.

## Outline Map 6.1

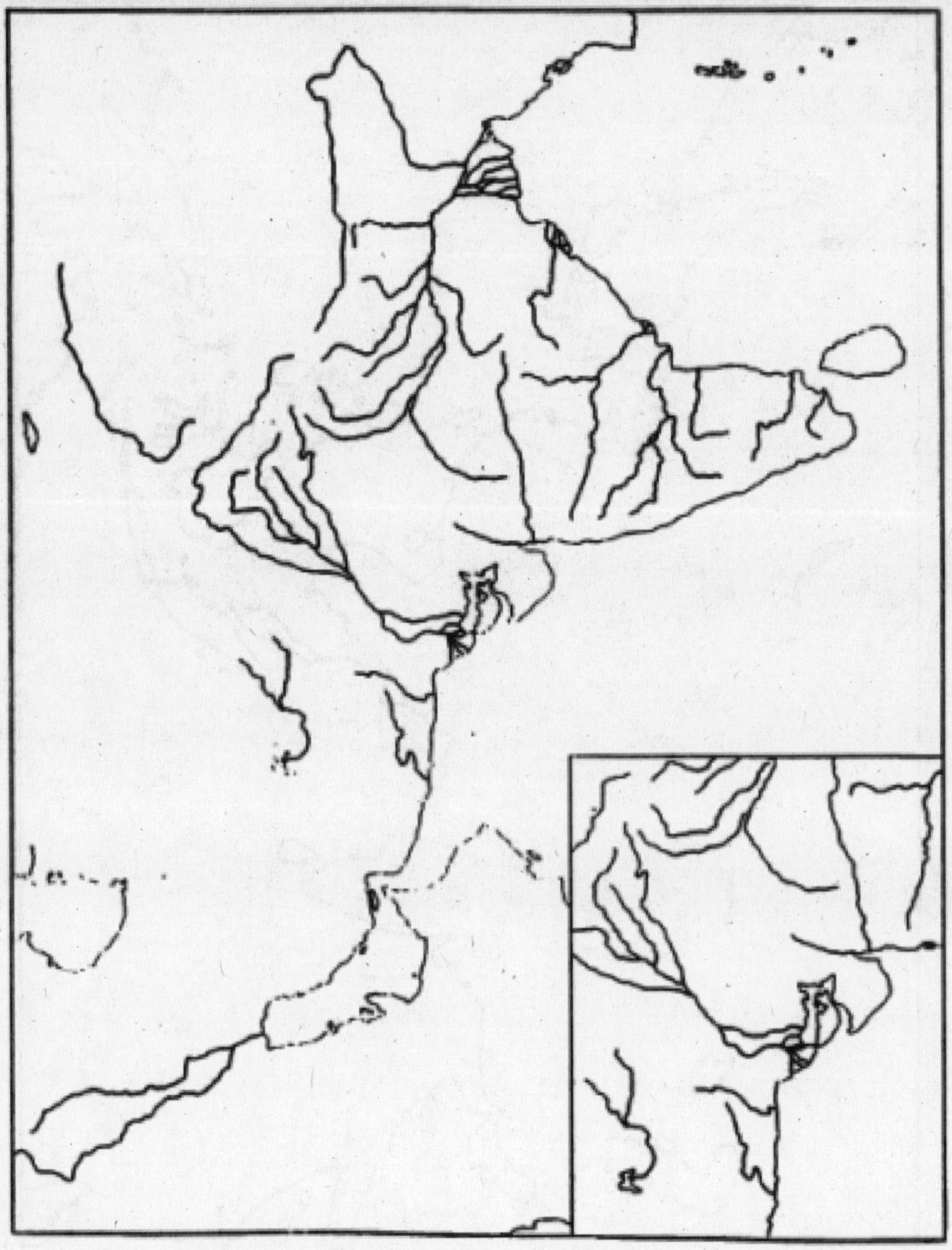

## Outline Map 6.2

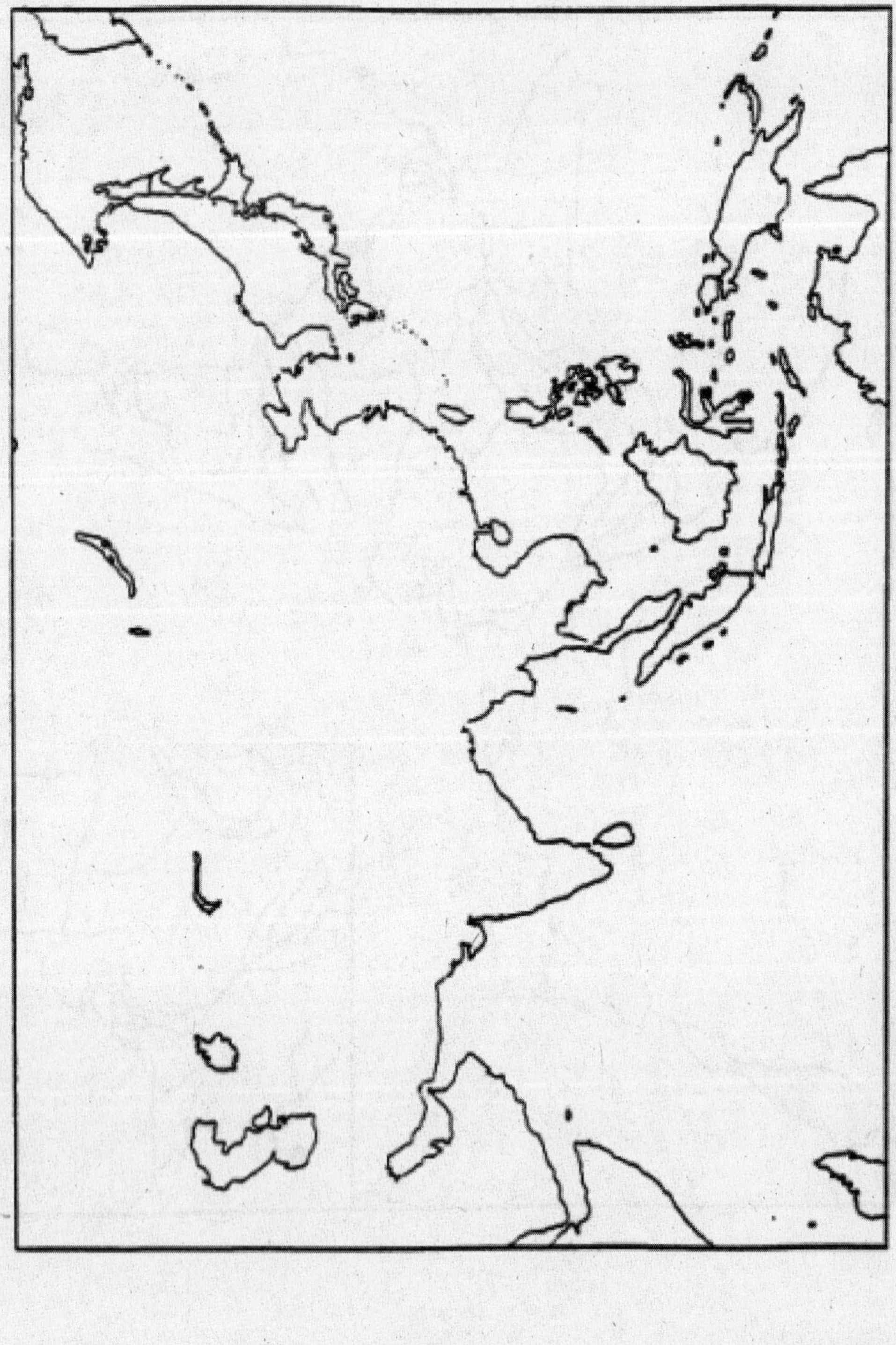

## FOCUS QUESTIONS

1. What were the major beliefs of Hinduism and Buddhism? How and/or where do they overlap or diverge?
2. What were the major political developments in India and Southeast Asia up to the year 600 C.E.?
3. How did Hinduism create and justify the social hierarchy in India?
4. How did Hinduism and Buddhism distinguish one's role and function in society based on gender?
5. How does the Indian caste system compare to other forms of social inequality (for example, slavery) studied in previous chapters?
6. How did the Indian subcontinent participate in the overall global trading system up to the year 600 C.E.?

## ANSWERS TO MULTIPLE-CHOICE QUESTIONS

1. b p. 169
2. a pp. 169–170
3. b p. 171
4. d p. 171
5. e pp. 171–172
6. c p. 172
7. a p. 173
8. a p. 170
9. c p. 166
10. c p. 176
11. e p. 176
12. c p. 183
13. a p. 183
14. e p. 183
15. d p. 184
16. d p. 175
17. b p. 176

# CHAPTER 7

# Networks of Communication and Exchange, 300 B.C.E.–600 C.E.

## BEFORE YOU BEGIN

AP World History organizes world history into five chronological eras, called periods. This "periodization" helps historians' understanding because it encourages organizing all historical information into different periods, which can then be compared against each other. Chapter 7 is the last chapter of the first period (what AP World History calls "Foundations," 8000 B.C.E. to 600 C.E.).

By the end of this chapter you should be able to do two types of historical tasks: (1) trace the chronological development of any major characteristic from the beginning to the end of the Foundations period, and (2) compare any characteristic from major civilizations during the Foundations period. These two skills are the basis of two types of AP World History essays: Change Over Time and Compare and Contrast. It also means that AP students must be careful not to forget information from previous chapters. A significant number of multiple-choice and essay questions on the AP exam require cross-cultural or cross-chronological comparisons. Simply memorizing the information in each chapter individually won't prepare you for such questions.

This chapter serves to wrap up the Foundations period by focusing on the historical information that doesn't neatly fit into any single previous chapter. For instance, the spread of ideas and religions is relevant to every chapter, not just China, Egypt, or India. Later in the course you'll be asked to compare historical trends across geographical and/or chronological periods. (e.g., "How did world trade patterns change from 1450–1914?" or "Compare the role religion played in supporting or weakening political authority in the Roman and Han Empires.") "Period Summarization" and "Name Five" tables will help you organize and remember what you've learned so far. These will be repeated for later chronological periods.

Remember that history is a human invention. Yes, there are objective, verifiable facts that comprise history, but there is also a significant amount of human *interpretation* involved. New facts may be discovered (or forgotten!), which in turn changes the ways humans interpret the past. A superior student can interpret a given set of historical facts in multiple ways, thus appreciating the validity of different interpretations even while disagreeing.

## LEARNING OBJECTIVES

After reading Chapter 7 and completing this study chapter, you should be able to:

- Explain how the Silk Road functioned as a conduit for goods, technology, and ideas, providing a link between far-flung empires and diverse peoples.
- Explain how the Indian Ocean system transformed the regions of Africa, the Middle East, China, and Southeast Asia into a major trade network operated by Chinese and Muslim sailors.
- Explain how even though the Sahara was a barrier to trade, it still permitted the transfer of vital goods and technology.

- Discuss how the migrations of the Bantu provided Africa with an underlying cultural unity and the legacy that this has left Africans.
- Discuss the impact the growth and spread of Buddhism and Christianity had on the peoples of Eurasia and Africa.

## IDENTIFICATIONS

Define each term and explain why it is significant, including any important dates.

**Silk Road**

**nomads**

**Parthians**

**stirrup**

**silk**

**caravan cities**

**camels**

**Indian Ocean maritime system**

**trans-Saharan caravan routes**

**Sahel**

**Ghana**

**sub-Saharan Africa**

**steppes**

**savanna**

**tropical rain forest**

**great traditions**

**small traditions**

**Bantu**

**salt trade**

**Armenia**

**Ethiopia**

___

___

## MULTIPLE-CHOICE QUESTIONS

Read the entire question, including *all* the possible answers. Then choose the *one* answer that best fits the question.

1. Which of the following statements about those who traveled along the Silk Road is *not* true?
   a. They were well respected by the local townspeople.
   b. They were nomads.
   c. They were secretive about their knowledge.
   d. They contributed more to the drawing together of the world than most kings.
   e. They seldom played a visible part in the rise and fall of kingdoms.
2. Emperor Wu of Han dynasty China sent out an expedition headed by General Zhang Jian in 128 B.C.E. to
   a. defeat the Xiongnu.
   b. make diplomatic overtures to the Scythians.
   c. explore trade possibilities with caravan cities.
   d. acquire paper-making technology from the Turks.
   e. hire Iranian dancing girls.
3. What did the Chinese want to import?
   a. A variety of Western goods, especially horses
   b. Porcelain
   c. Greek incense
   d. Cinnabar
   e. They only wanted to trade for cash, not to import anything.
4. Which of the following was *not* one of the technologies that originated in Central Asia?
   a. Chariot warfare
   b. The camel saddle
   c. The use of mounted bowmen
   d. Use of stirrups
   e. The yurt
5. The monsoon winds that facilitate sailing across the Indian Ocean were discovered by
   a. the Greek Hippalus.
   b. Zhang Jian.
   c. the Phoenicians.
   d. the Chinese.
   e. the peoples living in Africa, the Arabian peninsula, India, and the Malay Peninsula.
6. The island of Madagascar was settled by
   a. Africans only.
   b. Africans and Asians.
   c. Asians only.
   d. Polynesians.
   e. Phoenicians.

7. Evidence for the south-to-north adoption of camel use comes from
   a. written sources.
   b. studies of camel saddle design.
   c. studies of camel-breeding techniques.
   d. folk tales.
   e. rock art.
8. By the year 1 C.E., sub-Saharan Africa had become a distinct cultural region
   a. shaped by imperial conquest.
   b. characterized by an elite culture.
   c. due to the use of "great traditions" to unify it.
   d. due to its geography.
   e. unified by its many similar "small traditions."
9. When did outsiders gain control of the African continent and establish an elite culture?
   a. The Egyptians did during the New Kingdom
   b. The Romans did in the third century C.E.
   c. The Almoravids did around the year 1000 C.E.
   d. The Europeans did in the ninteenth century C.E.
   e. Never
10. Which of the following can probably be attributed to the desiccation of the Sahara?
    a. The Bantu migrations
    b. The emergence of the Old Kingdom of Egypt
    c. The fall of Rome
    d. The migration to Madagascar
    e. The domestication of the camel
11. Which of the following is *not* a valid theory about the use of iron in sub-Saharan Africa?
    a. Iron was discovered by the Hittites only.
    b. People from the Nile Valley spread it southward.
    c. Phoenician settlers brought it to North Africa, and from there it spread southward.
    d. Iron working could have developed in either West Africa or Meroë.
    e. Iron working technology came to Africa from Southeast Asia via Madagascar.
12. What evidence did pilgrims encounter that attested to the long history of Buddhist preaching and conversion along the Silk Road?
    a. The proliferation of Buddhist communities and monasteries in caravan cities
    b. The writings of Marco Polo
    c. The pillars erected by Ashoka
    d. The spread of Buddhism left no physical evidence
    e. The total lack of warfare in the area
13. Which of the following is an accurate description of the spread of religions in Eurasia before 600 C.E.?
    a. Christian and Jewish missionaries competed against each other in Europe for the same converts.
    b. Hinduism spread east along the Silk Road from India to China, while Buddhism spread west along the Silk Road from China to India.
    c. Monotheistic religions slowly replaced polytheism in South Asia, but polytheistic religions replaced monotheism in East Asia.
    d. Religions spread most commonly along the trade routes of the day, like the Silk Road and Roman road system.
    e. Religions spread most rapidly when unjust rulers tried to suppress rebellion to political oppression by unjust rulers.

# ESSAY QUESTIONS

Make an outline for each question, listing the major points you want to discuss. Then write your practice essay, following your outline carefully and making sure that you do not skip any of your major points. At this time, you will want to add the relevant dates and details that will make your essay persuasive and accurate.

## Change Over Time

Discuss the institution of the Silk Road. How did it work? Who ran it? What were some of the things that traveled along the Silk Road? How did it influence those who came into contact with it?

1. Describe the development and the mechanics of the trans-Saharan trading system. How did it differ from the maritime systems of the Mediterranean Sea and Indian Ocean?
2. Trace the spread of Buddhism from the second to the eighth century C.E. To what degree did the advent of the so-called great traditions such as Buddhism and Christianity completely displace local customs, traditions, and social formations? What was the role of the great traditions?
3. How did the relationship between religion and trade evolve up to the year 600 C.E.?
4. To what degree had humans' dependency on the environment changed from prehistoric times to 600 C.E.?

## Compare and Contrast

1. Compare and contrast the lifestyles and livelihoods of settled and nomadic peoples. What technologies did each employ? What geographic features did each have to address?
2. Compare and contrast the Mediterranean maritime world and the Indian Ocean maritime system prior to 600 C.E.

## General Essay

1. Rather than studying history by focusing on a particular civilization, this chapter organizes historical information differently. How does this organizational difference affect your view of history?

# COMPARISON CHARTS

Using information gathered from the text, fill in the blank areas of each chart with the relevant data pertaining to the regions and categories listed. (Not all blank areas will necessarily be equally complete.)

Chart 7.1

**CROSS-CULTURAL CONTACTS**

| | Geographic Regions | Livelihood | Housing | Technology | Possessions | Source of Wealth | Population | Government Structure | Contact with Opposite Group |
|---|---|---|---|---|---|---|---|---|---|
| Settled Peoples | | | | | | | | | |
| Nomads | | | | | | | | | |

Chart 7.2

TRADE ROUTES

| | Who Traded | Where | Transportation | Goods | Technology | Ideas | Impact |
|---|---|---|---|---|---|---|---|
| **Silk Road** | | | | | | | |
| **Indian Ocean Trading Basin** | | | | | | | |
| **Sub-Saharan African Routes** | | | | | | | |

## DIVERSITY AND DOMINANCE

After reading "Diversity and Dominance: The Indian Ocean Trading World" in your text, answer the following additional questions.

1. Can you guess where the author actually went? How are his biases apparent in his writing?
2. Do you see a correlation between geography and his use of terms like "wild-flesh eaters," "savages," and "cannibals"?

## INTERNET ASSIGNMENT

**Keywords:** **Ashoka's rock edicts**

**Mansa Musa Mali**

Many leaders actively promoted the spread of religion during their reigns. Use the above keywords to find websites about Ashoka and Mansa Musa Mali. You might want to consult the *History WIRED* image library on the Bulliet, *The Earth and Its Peoples* website (refer to the preface of this study guide for information on how to locate the Bulliet home page).

1. Both Ashoka and Mansa Musa helped to gain converts to Buddhism and Islam, respectively. What methods did they use?
2. How did their styles differ?
3. What were any long-term effects of their efforts?

## INTERNET EXPLORATION

The Silk Road was a major thoroughfare for trade during the empires of Rome and Han China. But many scholars think that the Silk Road's origins may date back much earlier, in fact, as much as two thousand years earlier. Use the keywords "Mummies Xinjiang Province" to see some evidence of early trade and travel along the legendary Silk Road. What kinds of people traveled the Silk Road, and why were scholars so surprised about their identity?

## MAP EXERCISES

On Outline Map 7.1, plot the following:

Silk Road

Rome

Indian Ocean

Malay Peninsula

India

Yellow River

Shade in these areas:

Roman Empire

Han dynasty China

Kushan Empire

Region of Mongols

Region of Turkic nomads

Show the spread of Buddhism by marking the original center in fifth century B.C.E. and shading in the areas to which Buddhism spread in these periods:

Fifth to third century B.C.E.

Third to second century B.C.E.

Second century B.C.E. to tenth century C.E.

On Outline Map 7.2, shade in the following:

Sub-Saharan Africa

East Africa

The historical kingdom of Ghana

## Outline Map 7.1

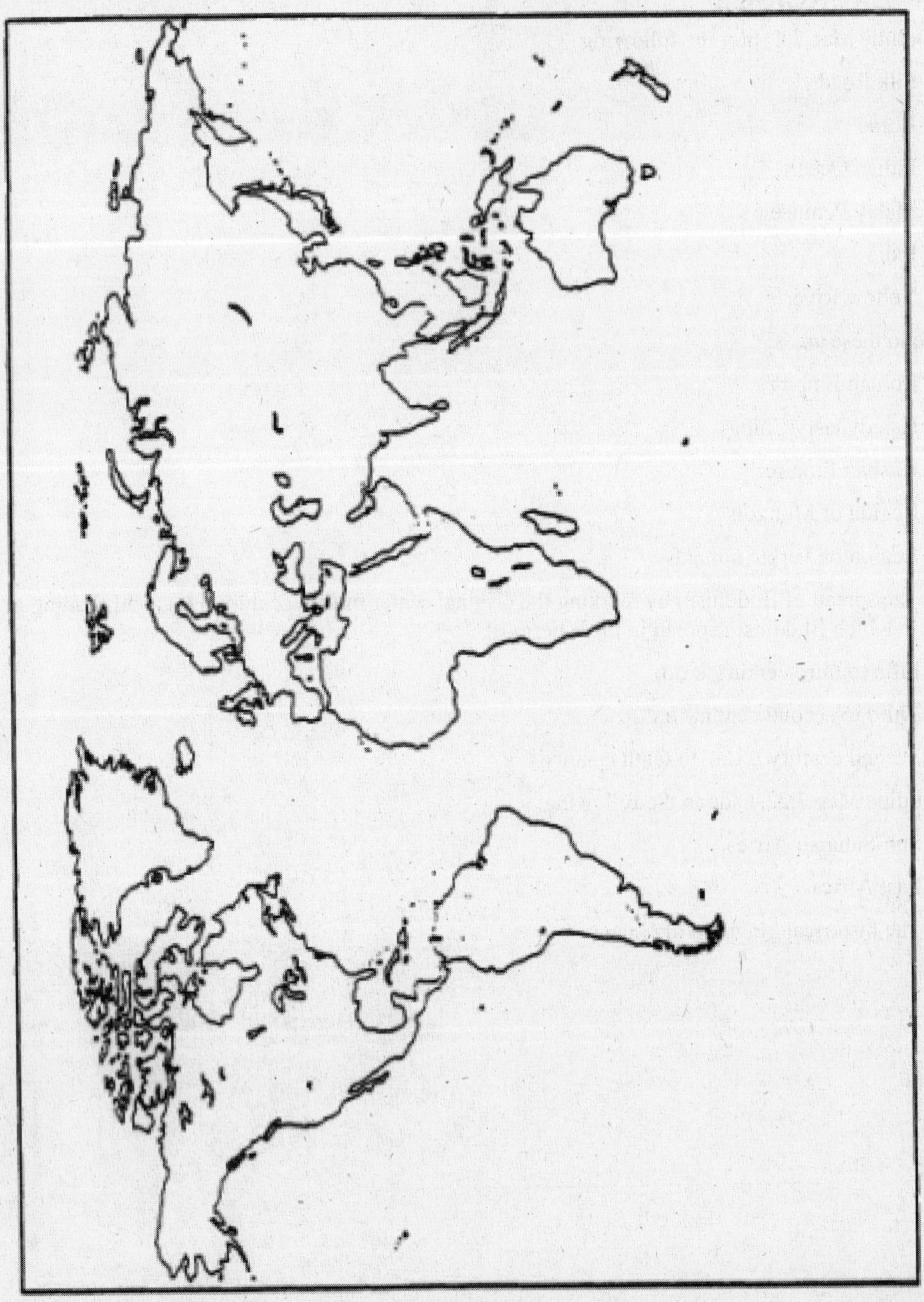

## Outline Map 7.2

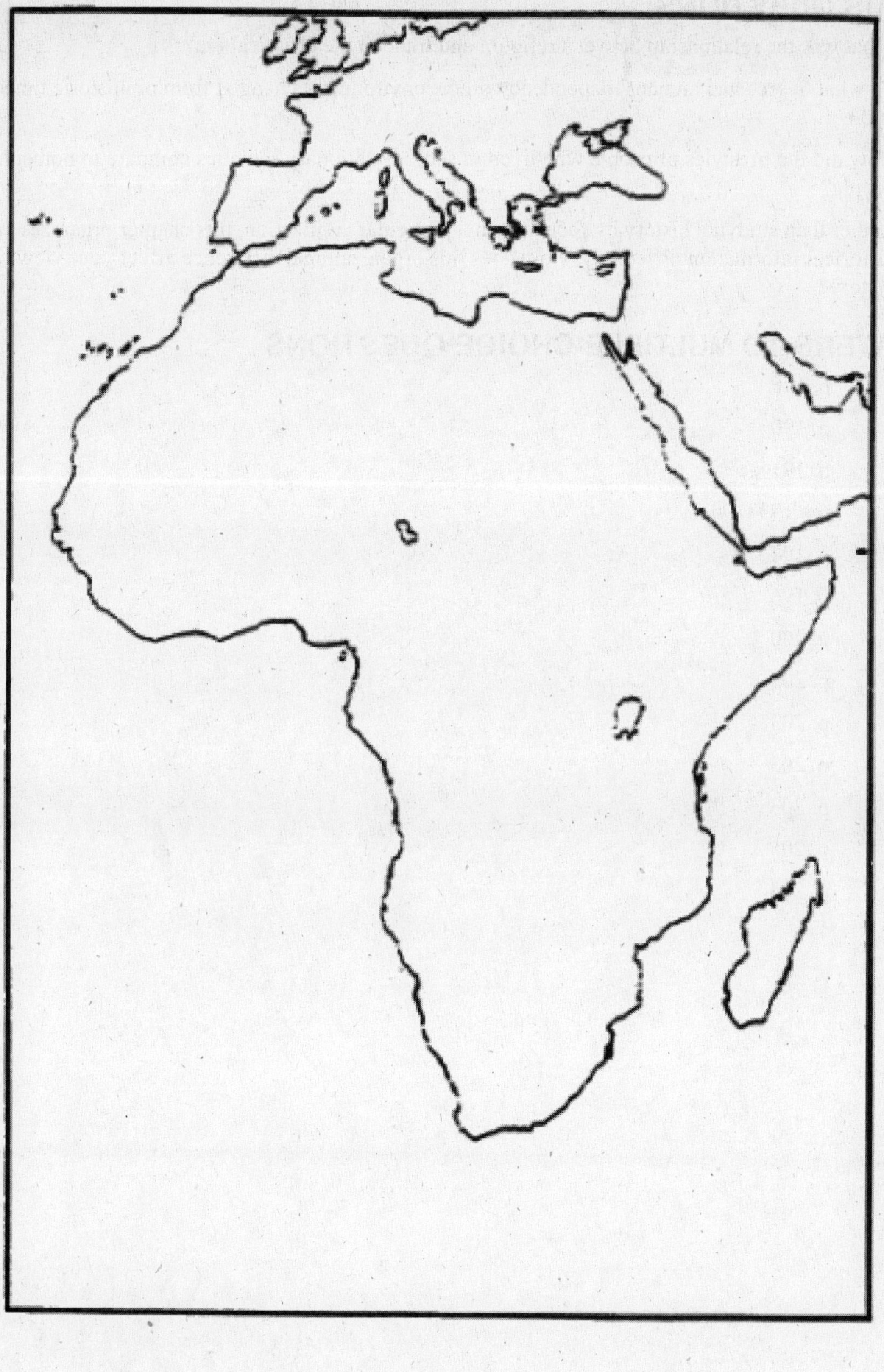

## FOCUS QUESTIONS

1. What was the relationship between religion and trade in the Classical era?
2. To what degree had humans' dependency on the environment changed from prehistoric times to 600 C.E.?
3. How did the lifestyles of people who lived in settled, stationary societies compare to nomadic people?
4. Rather than studying history by focusing on a particular civilization, this chapter organizes historical information differently. How does this organizational difference affect your view of history?

## ANSWERS TO MULTIPLE-CHOICE QUESTIONS

1. a p. 190
2. c p. 190
3. a p. 191
4. b pp. 193–194
5. e p. 194
6. b p. 196
7. e p. 200
8. e p. 202
9. d p. 203
10. b p. 203
11. e p. 203
12. a p. 205
13. d p. 204

CHAPTER 8

# The Rise of Islam, 600–1200

## BEFORE YOU BEGIN

Islam is possibly the most misunderstood religion in the United States. To gain a better understanding of Islam's role in AP World History, students need to understand that Islam not only has a well-known *religious* significance, but also a less well-known cultural role in influencing Muslims *and* people of other religions. The textbook will explore the longer-term impact of Islam and Muslims on other areas and peoples of the East in later chapters, but first take some time to focus on understanding Islam itself. Not only will this give you a better perspective on the past, but it may also enhance your understanding of current world affairs.

As you read, consider not only how Islam developed *as a religion*, but also how it became a political, social, and cultural identity. Then examine how Islam interacted with the people and cultures it encountered. This interaction is a major topic of the 600–1450 period, and it will reappear in later chapters.

## LEARNING OBJECTIVES

After reading Chapter 8 and completing this study chapter, you should be able to explain:

- How Islam originated, and how other traditions have influenced its development.
- How Islamic society developed secular rule, and how the institution of the caliphate evolved over time.
- What role the Quran and the hadith had in Muslim law and society.
- What influence Islam exerted on women, families, and slavery.
- How Islamic life differed in urban and rural areas.

## IDENTIFICATIONS

Define each term and explain why it is significant, including any important dates.

**Shi'ites**

______________________________________________

______________________________________________

**Sunnis**

______________________________________________

______________________________________________

**Sasanid Empire**

______________________________________________

______________________________________________

**Mecca**

**Muhammad**

**Ali**

**Abu Bakr**

**Muslim**

**Islam**

**Medina**

**umma**

**caliphate**

**Quran**

**A'isha**

**Umayyad caliphate**

**Abbasid caliphate**

**mamluks**

**ulama**

**Shari'a**

**hadith**

**madrasa**

## MULTIPLE-CHOICE QUESTIONS

Read the entire question, including *all* the possible answers. Then choose the *one* answer that best fits the question.

1. What role was *not* played by Arab pastoralists in the relationship between the Sasanid and Byzantine Empires?
   a. They were recruited as mercenaries.
   b. They were incorporated in the Sasanid and Byzantine governments as officials.
   c. They supplied camels and guides.
   d. They were merchants and organizers of caravans.
   e. They helped to protect the empires against invasion.
2. In the Muslim view, Judaism and Christianity were
   a. heretical religions.
   b. negligent in preserving God's word.
   c. useful only politically.
   d. threatening and should be destroyed.
   e. equal in value to Islam.

3. Why did Muslims change the direction of their prayer from Jerusalem to Mecca?
   a. They did so to differentiate between themselves and the Jews of Medina, who continued to practice Judaism.
   b. They made the change to show respect to the angel Jibra'il.
   c. It was a political move to strengthen them in the battle between Mecca and Medina.
   d. It was a compromise so that Muhammad and his followers could return to Mecca.
   e. They did not change it; it had always been directed toward Mecca.
4. The supremacy of the Medinan state was based on
   a. kinship.
   b. common faith in a single god.
   c. military might.
   d. trade.
   e. its ownership of the Ka'ba.
5. Which one of the following is *not* one of the Five Pillars of Islam?
   a. Avowal that there is only one god, and Muhammad is his messenger
   b. Prayer five times a day
   c. Fighting in Holy War, or Jihad
   d. Fasting during the lunar month of Ramadan
   e. Making pilgrimage to Mecca at least once during one's lifetime
6. To which factor can we attribute the success of the spread of the Muslim empire?
   a. The leniency of Islam toward Jews and Christians
   b. The warfare between the Sasanid and Byzantine Empires, which weakened these two empires
   c. The fact that the caliphs who guided the conquests were both sophisticated and inspired by Muhammad
   d. Muhammad's military genius
   e. A breakdown in trade on the Silk Road due to the rise of the Later Gupta Empire in India
7. Which of the following statements best describes the Arab Muslims' relationship to their subject peoples?
   a. They required all their subjects to convert, and they forced conversion by the sword if necessary.
   b. They required all their subjects to convert, but they offered ample financial rewards for conversion.
   c. There was an extensive missionary effort to encourage conversion.
   d. They required only Jews and Christians to convert.
   e. Arabs were a minority, and they had no incentive to promote cohesive missionary movements.
8. Which of the following factors did *not* contribute to the decline of the Umayyad dynasty?
   a. New converts to Islam felt that they deserved equal status with the privileged Arab warriors.
   b. The Umayyad ban on trade caused economic hardship.
   c. Pious Muslims felt that the Umayyad family behaved immorally.
   d. The Shi'ites and the Kharijites contested the Umayyad family's claim to rule on religious grounds.
   e. Other Arabs resented the influence that Syrian Arabs had in caliphal affairs.

9. As Islam developed, it
   a. remained untouched by outside influences.
   b. evolved but remained untouched by outside influences.
   c. was changed dramatically by local traditions.
   d. absorbed many "small traditions," within the "great tradition" of Islam.
   e. got lost within the "small traditions."
10. The hadith
   a. is a book of the Quran.
   b. provided a valuable supplement to the Quran, adding material on legal issues not covered there.
   c. is a collection of sayings that challenge the authority of the Quran.
   d. was a book of proper behavior for women, written by A'isha.
   e. provided legitimacy to the Shi'ite movement.
11. The practice of secluding and veiling women
   a. has its roots in Byzantine and Sasanid times.
   b. has its roots in the Quran.
   c. has its roots in the hadith.
   d. has its roots in one of the "little traditions" of the Muslim world.
   e. is actually a twentieth-century development and is a reaction to Western intrusion.
12. A hereditary slave society never developed in the Islamic world because
   a. slaves usually converted to Islam, often causing their masters to free them, and the offspring of slave women and Muslim men were free.
   b. the only people Muslims enslaved were Jews, Christians, and Zoroastrians, and they were scarce in the Middle East.
   c. slavery of Muslims was illegal according to the Quran.
   d. the mortality rate among slaves was so high, they rarely had children who lived to adulthood.
   e. all slavery was illegal according to the Quran.

## ESSAY QUESTIONS

Make an outline for each question, listing the major points you want to discuss. Then write your practice essay, following your outline carefully and making sure that you do not skip any of your major points. At this time, you will want to add the relevant dates and details that will make your essay persuasive and accurate.

### Change Over Time

1. Describe the religious atmosphere in Byzantium and the Arabian Peninsula before the rise of Islam. How did Islam change the outlook and behavior of the peoples from this region?
2. Describe the system of succession for the leadership of Islam. How did it originate and why? How did the schism occur, and what was its impact on Islam?
3. Discuss the decline of the institution of the caliphate. Why did it decline, and what were the results of that decline?
4. How did Islam become a cultural and economic unifying force between 600 and1200 C.E.?
5. What were the major turning points in the development of the caliphate from the beginnings of Islam through 1258 C.E.?

6. What do the Islamic artistic, scientific, and technological accomplishments indicate about Islamic civilization?

## Compare and Contrast

1. How did the Abbasid caliphate differ in style and substance from the Umayyad caliphate?

# COMPARISON CHARTS

Using information gathered from the text, fill in the blank areas of each chart with the relevant data pertaining to the regions and categories listed. (Not all blank areas will necessarily be used.)

Chart 8.1

JUDAISM, CHRISTIANITY, AND ISLAM

| | God(s) | Afterlife | Sin and Judgment | Practices | Leaders | Political Views | Texts | Society | Law |
|---|---|---|---|---|---|---|---|---|---|
| Judaism | | | | | | | | | |
| Christianity | | | | | | | | | |
| Islam | | | | | | | | | |

## Chart 8.2

### UMAYYAD AND ABBASID

| | Dates | Capital | Founder(s) | Outlook | Style | Challengers to Conquer | Role of Religion | Decline |
|---|---|---|---|---|---|---|---|---|
| **Umayyad** | | | | | | | | |
| **Abbasid** | | | | | | | | |

## DIVERSITY AND DOMINANCE

After reading "Diversity and Dominance: Beggars, Con Men, and Singing-girls" in your text, answer the following additional questions.

1. What was the lifestyle of the beggars and con men, and how is that reflected in the poem?
2. Why might these people be so amusing to travelers?
3. How do singing-girls differ from other Muslim women? Why? Do you think that this gives them more freedom in Muslim society or less freedom?

## INTERNET ASSIGNMENT

**Keywords:** **Richard the Lionheart**

**Saladin**

During the Crusades, and sometimes even since then, Christians and Muslims have dehumanized each other during times of conflict. Truthfully, both sides contributed vast resources to the passionate cause of the Crusades, and both sides created heroes. Two heroes on opposite sides that managed to gain the respect even of the "enemy" were Richard I of England (or Richard the Lionheart) and Saladin, a Kurd fighting on the Muslim side. Use the above keywords to find websites about these two men. You might want to consult the *History WIRED* image library on the Bulliet, *The Earth and Its Peoples* website (refer to the preface of this study guide for information on how to locate the Bulliet home page).

1. How were the aims of these two men similar? How were they different?
2. Does the way their portraits were drawn in the past influence our opinion of them today?

## INTERNET EXPLORATION

People living in the West view the veiling of Muslim women as repressive and demeaning. Muslims, including Muslim women, often do not share this view. Explore Muslim and non-Muslim opinions on veiling by using the keywords "women Islam veil" and "hijab." Why do Westerners have issues with veiling? Why do many Muslim women voluntarily practice veiling? Does the practice of "hijab" (modest dress and behavior) apply only to women? How do people who practice veiling view the clothing styles of Western peoples?

## MAP EXERCISE

On Outline Map 8.1, shade the areas of Muslim expansion under Muhammad during these periods:

622–632

632–661

661–750

Outline the areas controlled by the following:

Umayyad caliphate

Abbasid caliphate

Muslims in Cordoba, Spain

## Outline Map 8.1

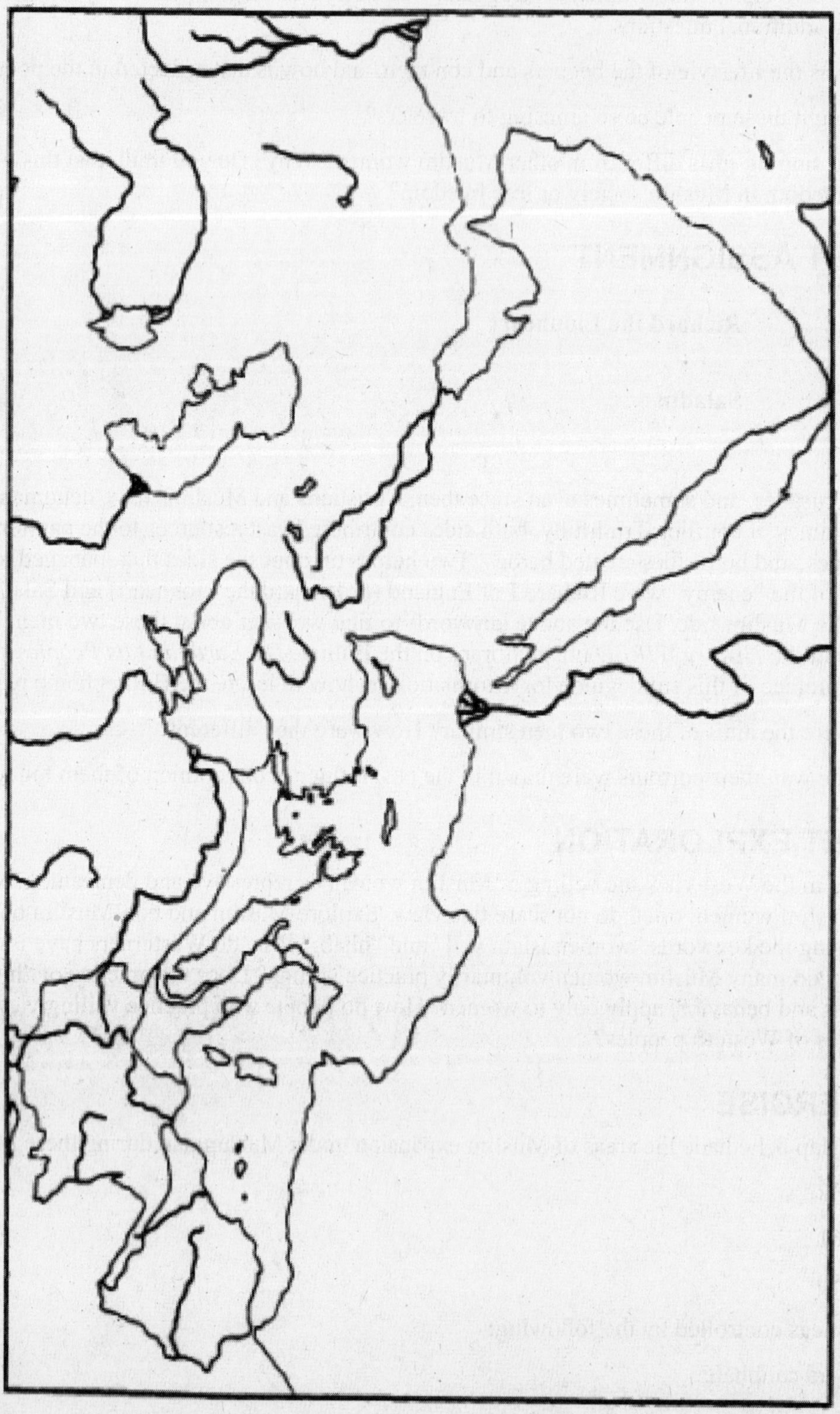

## FOCUS QUESTIONS

1. How did Islam become a cultural and economic unifying force between 600 and 1200 C.E.?
2. What were the major turning points in the development of the caliphate from the beginnings of Islam through 1258 C.E.?
3. What do the Islamic artistic, scientific, and technological accomplishments indicate about Islamic civilization?

## ANSWERS TO MULTIPLE-CHOICE QUESTIONS

1. b p. 216
2. b p. 219
3. a p. 219
4. b p. 220
5. c p. 220
6. c p. 221
7. e p. 222
8. b p. 222
9. d p. 227
10. b pp. 227–228
11. a p. 230
12. a p. 232

CHAPTER 9

# Christian Societies Emerge in Europe, 600–1200

## BEFORE YOU BEGIN

Europe after the fall of the Roman Empire has often been characterized as the Dark Ages. The textbook challenges this common overgeneralization. One of the challenges of studying Europe during this period is trying to compare Eastern and Western Europe. You'll find similarities (Christianity spread throughout) and differences (Roman Catholicism versus Eastern Orthodoxy) simultaneously. Politically, the Roman Empire fragmented into regional states, but the Byzantine Empire carried on, in some ways even better than before. The economic and demographic health of Europe declined, but new cultural patterns emerged even in the midst of disorder. Look for several interesting contrasts comparing geographic regions or long-term trends that make for great Change Over Time questions.

## LEARNING OBJECTIVES

After reading Chapter 9 and completing this study chapter, you should be able to:

- Explain how European society evolved from the remnants of the Roman Empire, eventually combining Roman tradition, Christianity, and Germanic culture into a distinctive society.
- Describe what role the Latin Church played in Western Europe, and how it compared with the role played by the Byzantine Church.
- Explain how the paths of the former Western Roman Empire and the Byzantine Empire diverged and why.
- Describe what role technology and improvements in agriculture played in the development of the European economy.
- Explain how Kievan Russia developed both in conjunction with Western Europe and Byzantium, yet developed distinctive characteristics.

## IDENTIFICATIONS

Define each term and explain why it is significant, including any important dates.

**Charlemagne (Charles the Great)**

______________________________________________

______________________________________________

**investiture controversy**

______________________________________________

______________________________________________

**medieval**

______________________________________________

______________________________________________

**monasticism**

**Byzantine Empire**

**Kievan Russia**

**schism**

**manor/manorialism**

**horse collar**

**serfs**

**Crusades**

**nobles**

**feudalism**

**fief**

**pilgrimage**

**vassal**

**papacy**

**Holy Roman Empire**

**Rule of Benedict**

**Hagia Sophia**

**Cyrillic**

## MULTIPLE-CHOICE QUESTIONS

Read the entire question, including *all* the possible answers. Then choose the *one* answer that best fits the question.

1. The crowning of Charlemagne as emperor of the Romans by the pope symbolized
   a. the rise of a new Roman Empire.
   b. a shift in focus away from the Mediterranean and toward northern Germanic Europe.
   c. a shift away from secular rule and toward theocracy.
   d. the new power of the papacy.
   e. Charlemagne's own desire to be the pope.
2. Why is the period in Europe between 500 C.E. and 1300 C.E. called the Middle Ages?
   a. It came between the Greco-Roman civilization and the Renaissance.
   b. Europe, at this time, was controlled by peoples in its central area rather than by the people of the Mediterranean, as it had been in the past.
   c. It was the beginning of the rise of the middle class.
   d. Europe was invaded by Muslim nomads from the Middle East.
   e. It comes from the Buddhist term *the Middle Days of the Law*.

3. Which of the following was *not* a unifying force in the chaotic remains of the Western Roman Empire?
   a. Germanic family-based law
   b. The Roman judicial system
   c. Effective rulers, such as Charlemagne
   d. The Christian church
   e. Slavic religious tradition
4. Which of the following statements best characterizes the influence of Roman traditions in Byzantium?
   a. Byzantium carried on the traditions of Rome, including Christianity, almost without interruption.
   b. Byzantium made a dramatic break with Roman tradition, as did Western Europe.
   c. Byzantium was influenced so much by Islam that it gradually rejected Roman traditions.
   d. Byzantium carried on the traditions of Rome but mixed them freely with Germanic traditions.
   e. Byzantines became Muslim.
5. Why is it paradoxical that women ruled the Byzantine Empire together with their husbands from 1028 to 1056?
   a. Roman family structure was traditionally loose, and women had been comparatively active in public life.
   b. Byzantine women increasingly found themselves confined to their homes and required to veil themselves in public.
   c. The law code gave women no political rights.
   d. The patriarch said that women should work only in the home.
   e. Women usually ruled alone.
6. The growth of the great fortified manors was prompted by all of the following factors *except*
   a. religious wars.
   b. isolation due to poor communication networks.
   c. political insecurity.
   d. warfare and instability between different powerful local families.
   e. vulnerability to attack by the Vikings.
7. How did improvements in armor dictate changes as to who could become a mounted knight?
   a. As armor became heavier, only those who were particularly physically fit could fight with it on.
   b. As armor became one of the items imported from China, only those in trading cities or the sons of merchants could obtain it.
   c. When the church sent soldiers on crusade, they issued the best armor only to those they deemed spiritually fit.
   d. As armor became more effective, fewer soldiers were required, and so only a select few were chosen to fight.
   e. As armor became more expensive, only knights who had financial support from land revenues could afford to outfit themselves properly.
8. Which of the following statements about noblewomen in medieval Europe is *not* true?
   a. Noblewomen became enmeshed in the tangle of feudal obligations through marriage.
   b. Noblewomen lived powerless, sheltered lives.
   c. Noblewomen were guarded by noblemen as part of their prized possessions.
   d. Some noblewomen exercised real power, administering their husband's lands when they were away at war.
   e. Noblewomen could own property.

9. What was the investiture controversy?
   a. A disagreement about the standards for choosing the pope
   b. A conflict between popes and kings regarding control of ecclesiastical offices
   c. A disagreement about how knights should be chosen
   d. A conflict between the various kings regarding the legality of parliaments
   e. A debate regarding how to invest papal income
10. Most ancient works in Latin would have disappeared if
    a. some classical person had not hidden hundreds of them away in caves.
    b. ninth-century monks had not copied them.
    c. Muslim invaders had not carried them off to their homelands as booty.
    d. they had not become popular as relics.
    e. they had not been translated into Chinese.
11. Why did Kievan Russians decide to adopt Orthodox Christianity?
    a. They were impressed by the magnificence of Constantinople.
    b. They were betrayed by Jewish Khazars and so rejected Judaism.
    c. The Slavs revolted, demanding they adopt Orthodox Christianity.
    d. The Roman pope did not support the rule of Vladimir II.
    e. Actually, they chose Islam instead.
12. Which of the following technological innovations probably did *not* play a significant role in the launching of the economy of Western Europe after the year 1000?
    a. An improved horse collar
    b. The importation of a superior plow from the Mediterranean
    c. The development of a plow that both cut and turned the soil
    d. The use of teams of horses rather than oxen
    e. The use of iron horseshoes
13. Which of the following is *not* one of the reasons usually offered by historians for the Crusades?
    a. The church wanted to cut down on warfare between Christian lords and redirect it toward enemies of the church.
    b. Ambitious lords were looking for new lands to conquer.
    c. Italian merchants wanted to increase trade.
    d. The pope wanted to recapture the Holy Land.
    e. Younger sons of the nobility wanted land and titles that would not be available to them at home.
14. How did the culture of Western Europe differ from Eastern Europe in the centuries after Rome's fall?
    a. Western Europe focused more on religion, while Eastern Europe emphasized more scientific accomplishments.
    b. Eastern Europe sank into centuries of cultural stagnation, while Western Europe experienced a revival of Rome's former imperial glory.
    c. Western European social classes became more clearly defined due to the influence of feudalism, while Eastern Europe's social classes allowed for a greater degree of mobility.
    d. Women in Western Europe were far more likely to be educated than were women in Eastern Europe.
    e. Religious practices of Western and Eastern Europe slowly diverged as the tensions between the pope and patriarch grew.

15. How did Western and Eastern Europe compare politically from 600 to 1200 C.E.?
    a. Eastern Europe relied on protection from Slavic princes to the North, while Western Europe became a unified political force under Charlemagne.
    b. Western Europe fragmented into dozens of provincial states, while Eastern Europe remained unified under Byzantium's leadership.
    c. Religious authorities in Western Europe lost political influence, while Orthodox patriarchs in Eastern Europe gained political influence.
    d. The investiture controversy was a constant source of conflict for Eastern Europe, but it was resolved by the Treaty of Verdun in 843 C.E. for western princes.
    e. The Holy Roman Empire slowly consolidated the lands previously ruled by Rome, while Byzantium slowly descended from imperial glory to a mere shadow of its former status.

## ESSAY QUESTIONS

Make an outline for each question, listing the major points you want to discuss. Then write your practice essay, following your outline carefully and making sure that you do not skip any of your major points. At this time, you will want to add the relevant dates and details that will make your essay persuasive and accurate.

### Change Over Time

1. Describe the transition from Roman society to medieval society. Pay special attention to social, economic, religious, and political issues.

2. Discuss the growth of cities and the rebirth of trade. What led to these developments, and how was society affected?

3. The Crusades were a major event in Europe of the Middle Ages. Why were they conducted, who benefited from them, and how did they affect Christian-Muslim relations?

4. What new political systems emerged in Europe after the fall of Rome? How consistent were these systems, and what major variations were there?

5. How and why did Christianity spread throughout Europe up to 1200 C.E.?

6. Analyze the degree to which Christianity diverged into two branches: Eastern Orthodoxy and Roman Catholicism.

### Compare and Contrast

1. Compare and contrast the development of Latin Europe, Byzantium, and Kievan Russia, paying special attention to religion and political unity.

2. What improvements were made to help increase agricultural production in Western Europe? How did these compare with agricultural techniques in Byzantium?

3. How does the economic, social, and political structure of Europe compare to the previous era under the Roman Empire?

### General Essay

1. Discuss the conflicts between religious and secular authorities in medieval Europe. What form did the disagreements take, over what issues were they generated, and how were they resolved?

## COMPARISON CHARTS

Using information gathered from the text, fill in the blank areas of each chart with the relevant data pertaining to the regions and categories listed. (Not all blank areas will necessarily be equally complete.)

**Chart 9.1**

**FROM ROMAN EMPIRE TO GERMANIC KINGDOMS**

| | Regional Focus | Law | Political Structure | Church | Economy | Status and Role of Women | Decline |
|---|---|---|---|---|---|---|---|
| **Rome** | | | | | | | |
| **Germanic Kingdoms** | | | | | | | |

## Chart 9.2

### LATIN WEST AND BYZANTINE EMPIRE

| | Unity | Political Structure | Religious Structure | Social Structure | Trade and Economics | Status of Women | Decline |
|---|---|---|---|---|---|---|---|
| Latin West | | | | | | | |
| Byzantine Empire | | | | | | | |

## DIVERSITY AND DOMINANCE

After reading "Diversity and Dominance: Archbishop Adalbert of Hamburg and the Christianization of the Scandinavians and the Slavs" in your text, answer the following additional questions.

1. Why does Adam of Bremen focus on the careers of Archbishop Adalbert, and then the caesars and popes connected with Emperor Henry and Pope Benedict?
2. How was Adalbert's arrogance viewed by the church? How do you think Adam of Bremen viewed it?

## INTERNET ASSIGNMENT

**Keywords:** **Viking ships**

**Hagia Sophia**

The contributions of the Vikings and the Byzantines, or Eastern Romans, have helped to form today's Western culture; they were, however, vastly different societies. Use the keywords above to find websites about Viking ships and the Hagia Sophia. You might want to consult the *History WIRED* image library on the Bulliet, *The Earth and Its Peoples* website (refer to the preface of this study guide for information on how to locate the Bulliet home page).

1. Why are Viking ships the perfect symbol of Viking society?
2. How is Byzantine society reflected in the Hagia Sophia?
3. How have these structures been preserved until modern times?

## INTERNET EXPLORATION

Mystery and magic surround the written language of early Germanic peoples. Where are runes from? What do they mean? Are they magical? Use the keyword "runes" to learn more, or go to http://www.pbs.org/wgbh/nova/vikings/runes2.html to learn more about runes and their uses. As a bonus, learn to write your name in runes.

## MAP EXERCISE

On Outline Map 9.1 (provided below), trace the routes of the following:

Vikings

Muslims

Ostrogoths

First Crusade

Second Crusade

Third Crusade

Fourth Crusade

Shade in the boundaries of the following:

Islamic world, 600–800

Crusader kingdoms in the East

Christian lands, 300–600

Christian lands, 600–800

## Outline Map 9.1

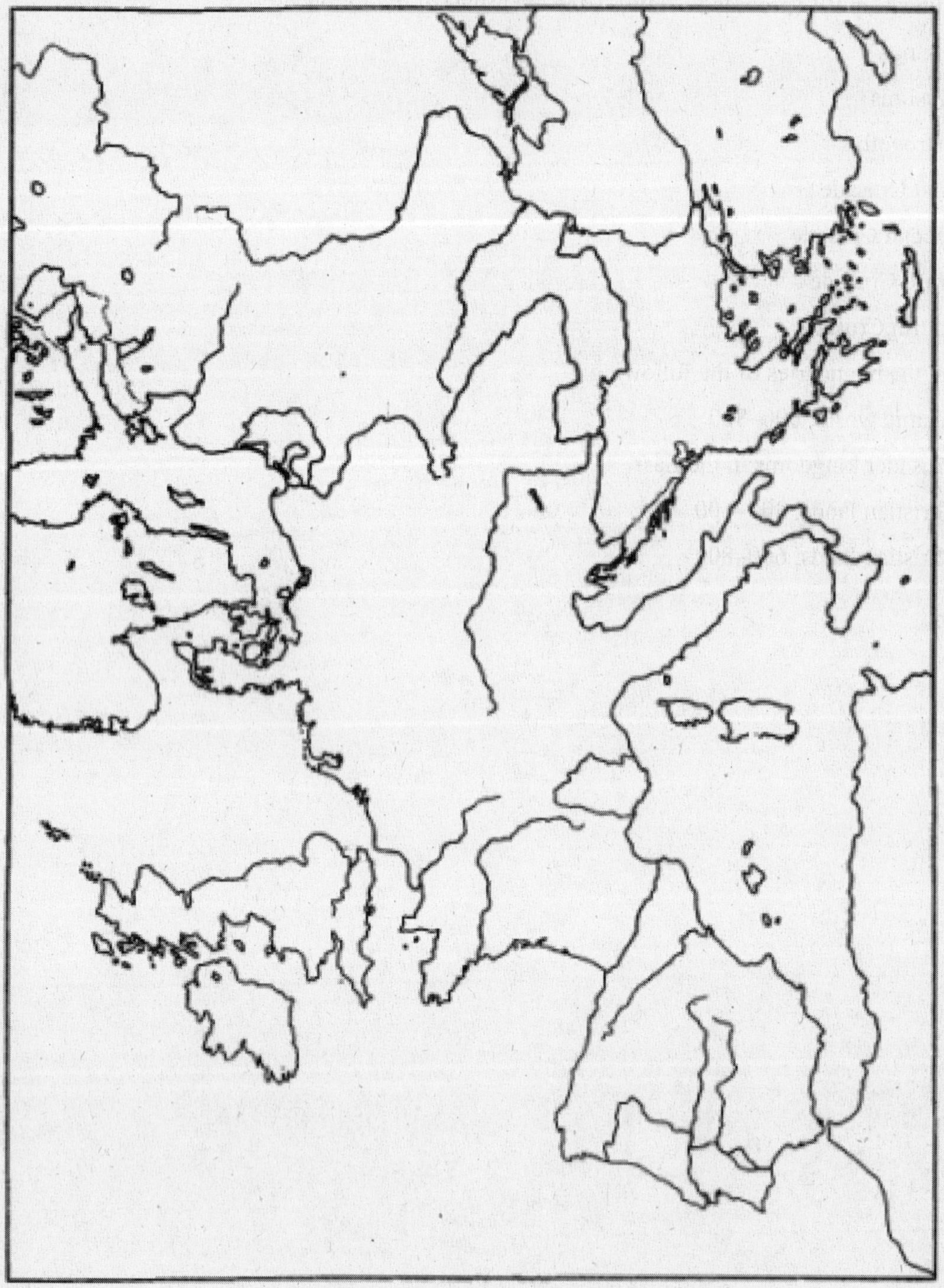

## FOCUS QUESTIONS

1. What new political systems emerged in Europe after the fall of Rome? How consistent were these systems, and what major variations were there?
2. How and why did Christianity spread throughout Europe up to 1200 C.E.?
3. How does the economic, social, and political structure of Europe compare to the previous era under the Roman Empire?
4. Describe the process by which Christianity diverged into two branches: Eastern Orthodoxy and Roman Catholicism.

## ANSWERS TO MULTIPLE-CHOICE QUESTIONS

1. b p. 240
2. a p. 240
3. e p. 244
4. a p. 240
5. b p. 243
6. a p. 246
7. e p. 247
8. b p. 247
9. b p. 252
10. b p. 253
11. a p. 256
12. b p. 257
13. d pp. 259–260
14. e p. 249
15. b p. 263

CHAPTER 10

# Inner and East Asia, 600–1200

## BEFORE YOU BEGIN

In the post-classical era after the fall of the Han dynasty, Chinese society and culture were defined less by political developments than by religious and philosophical belief systems. Even after imperial rule was restored with the Sui and Tang dynasties, cultural forces influenced East Asia as much (or more) than political forces did. One of the main points of this chapter is to examine how these cultural influences interacted, sometimes working together in concert, sometimes moderating the influence of each other.

## LEARNING OBJECTIVES

After reading Chapter 10 and completing this study chapter, you should be able to:

- Explain how the Sui and Tang dynasties of China rose, fell, and influenced both later dynasties and the peoples around them.
- Discuss how Buddhism was received in the various East Asian and Central Asian countries, how it changed them, and in turn how they adapted and controlled it.
- Describe how the lifestyles of nomadic and sedentary peoples differed, and how geography influenced their choice of lifestyle.
- Explain how the Song dynasty differed from earlier dynasties, and how it changed the outlook of the Chinese and influenced society.
- Describe what role Chinese culture played in the development of Korea, Japan, and Vietnam, and how each of them both adapted Chinese culture and retained their own distinct traditions.
- Explain how the role of cities developed during this period and the kinds of economic and cultural activity that took place in cities.
- Discuss the nature and degree of trade networks throughout Eurasia.
- Discuss the significance of the artistic, scientific, and technological developments of the Tang and Song dynasties.

## IDENTIFICATIONS

Define each term and explain why it is significant, including any important dates.

**Chang'an**

______________________________________________________________________

______________________________________________________________________

**Grand Canal**

______________________________________________________________________

______________________________________________________________________

**Tang Empire**

**Li Shimin**

**Tibet**

**tributary system**

**Mahayana Buddhism**

**bubonic plague**

**Uighurs**

**Kamakura shogunate**

**Song Empire**

**junk**

**gunpowder**

**Zen**

**shamanism**

**Neo-Confucianism**

**Koryo**

**Shinto**

**examination system**

**footbinding**

**movable type**

**Fujiwara**

***The Tale of Genji***

**Champa rice**

## MULTIPLE-CHOICE QUESTIONS

Read the entire question, including *all* the possible answers. Then choose the *one* answer that best fits the question.

1. The purpose of the Grand Canal was to
   a. facilitate trade and communication within China.
   b. enhance China's ability to protect itself from foreign invasion.
   c. bring students into the capital to take the imperial examinations.
   d. irrigate rice paddies in northern China.
   e. increase immigration from Korea.
2. The Sui Empire lasted such a short time because
   a. its rulers were not driven toward expansion.
   b. it was invaded by "barbarians."
   c. it was exhausted by its extraordinary pace of expansion and overcentralization.
   d. the last emperor, Yangdi, was an evil man.
   e. a series of violent storms flooded the capital city, Xian.
3. Which of the following is a belief of Mahayana Buddhism?
   a. Life is suffering.
   b. Bodhisattvas have postponed nirvana to help others achieve enlightenment.
   c. All people need to renounce their old customs and gods.
   d. Monks should retire to monasteries and have no contact with other people.
   e. Only men could be practicing Buddhists.
4. Which of the following is *not* one of the ways that Buddhist institutions allied themselves with the Tang imperial family?
   a. Monastic leaders openly supported women as emperors.
   b. Monastic leaders counseled aristocrats to support the imperial princes.
   c. Monastic leaders prayed for aspiring imperial princes.
   d. Monks preached on behalf of the imperial princes.
   e. Monasteries contributed money to imperial war chests.
5. How did the bubonic plague reach East Asia?
   a. It was brought by European Crusaders to the Middle East and then transmitted along the Silk Road to China.
   b. It traveled along the Grand Canal.
   c. It came from sub-Saharan Africa, spread to India, and then went by sea to Chang'an.
   d. It started in Spain, then traveled by sea to Africa, and was carried from China to Japan.
   e. It came along the sea route linking the Red Sea and Persian Gulf with Canton.
6. The Uighurs were famous as merchants and
   a. monks.
   b. warriors.
   c. diplomats.
   d. mathematicians.
   e. scribes.
7. The most dramatic change in the status of Chinese women during the Song dynasty was manifested by
   a. the introduction of slavery.
   b. footbinding.
   c. the admittance of women into the military.
   d. veiling.
   e. the introduction of education for women.

8. Why did the Song Empire look east and south for allies?
   a. To the west was uninhabited desert.
   b. Korea, Japan, and Vietnam had been settled originally by Chinese people and so were very similar to China.
   c. Like Song China, the regions to the east and south formed one Confucian region.
   d. Areas north and west of China were strongly oriented toward Buddhism.
   e. It needed the people of these regions for military support.
9. Why was rice growing well suited to Confucian ideology?
   a. It demanded the cooperation of large kin groups.
   b. Rice was white, symbolizing ideological purity.
   c. Rice was easy to weigh and transport and so made taxation more efficient.
   d. Growing rice was so time-consuming that peasants had no time to study for the imperial examinations.
   e. Only women grew rice, and this increased their subordinate role.
10. Where was movable type originally developed?
   a. Europe
   b. China
   c. Japan
   d. Korea
   e. Vietnam
11. During the eighth century Japan can best be described as
   a. backward and underdeveloped.
   b. a "little China."
   c. a "little Korea."
   d. warlike.
   e. a major Buddhist center, perhaps surpassing China.
12. The concept of the Mandate of Heaven was not important in Japan because
   a. Japan was less warlike than China.
   b. Confucianism was less accepted in Japan.
   c. Japanese rulers always came from the same family.
   d. the concept was never transmitted to Japan by Korea.
   e. the Japanese didn't believe in karma.
13. The combination of loneliness, free time, and writing encouraged Japanese women to
   a. produce an outpouring of poetry, diaries, and novels.
   b. get married.
   c. form alliances with each other.
   d. become wandering nuns.
   e. commit suicide.
14. The early Annamese were probably *not* ahead of the Chinese in their
   a. mastery of certain forms of ceramics.
   b. use of draft animals in agriculture.
   c. military tactics.
   d. metalworking.
   e. retention of a high status for women.

15. Which of the following statements best characterizes the beliefs of Neo-Confucianism?
    a. The Mandate of Heaven favors the Song emperors.
    b. This life on earth is unimportant compared to the afterlife.
    c. Humans are essentially good and reasonable.
    d. Korea and Japan should be included in "Greater China."
    e. Familial responsibilities should always come before military duties.

## ESSAY QUESTIONS

Make an outline for each question, listing the major points you want to discuss. Then write your practice essay, following your outline carefully and making sure that you do not skip any of your major points. At this time, you will want to add the relevant dates and details that will make your essay persuasive and accurate.

### Change Over Time

1. Discuss the cultural, social, political, and economic impact of Buddhism on East Asia, using specific examples from both China and Japan.
2. Discuss the various ways in which China influenced the rest of East Asia. In what ways did Korea, Japan, and Vietnam remain culturally distinct?
3. How did the Sui and Tang dynasties of China rise, fall, and influence both later dynasties and the peoples around them?
4. How was Buddhism received in the various East Asian and Central Asian countries? How did it change as it spread to the various regions?
5. What role did Chinese culture play in the development of Korea, Japan, and Vietnam? How did each of them both adapt elements of Chinese culture and retain their own distinct traditions?
6. How did the role of cities develop during this period? What kinds of economic and cultural activity took place in cities?
7. Assess the validity of this statement, "Eurasia developed an integrated network of economic activity by the year 1200 C.E."
8. How significant were the artistic, scientific, and technological developments of the Tang and Song dynasties?

### Compare and Contrast

1. Compare and contrast the roles and status of men and women in Song dynasty China. Be sure to consider men and women of all classes.
2. Compare and contrast the lifestyles of nomadic and sedentary peoples. How did geography influence their lifestyles?

### General Essay

1. Why *didn't* China experience an industrial revolution before 1200 C.E.?

## COMPARISON CHARTS

Using information gathered from the text, fill in the blank areas of each chart with the relevant data pertaining to the regions and categories listed. (Not all blank areas will necessarily be equally complete.)

## Chart 10.1

### TWO APPROACHES

| | Dates | Social Structure | Trade and Economy | Military | External Threats | Internal Threats | Status of Women | Religion | Technology |
|---|---|---|---|---|---|---|---|---|---|
| Tang Dynasty | | | | | | | | | |
| Song Dynasty | | | | | | | | | |

## Chart 10.2
## CHINA, CENTRAL ASIA, KOREA, JAPAN, AND ANNAM

| | Political Structure | Social Structure | Examination System | Confucianism | Buddhism | Status of Women | Economy and Trade | Technology |
|---|---|---|---|---|---|---|---|---|
| China | | | | | | | | |
| Central Asia | | | | | | | | |
| Korea | | | | | | | | |
| Japan | | | | | | | | |
| Annam | | | | | | | | |

## DIVERSITY AND DOMINANCE

After reading "Diversity and Dominance: Law and Society in Tang China" in your text, answer the following additional questions.

1. What types of crimes does the Tang Law Code seem to concern itself most with? What types of crimes seem to be missing? Why?
2. Why do you think that the peasants suffered such a terrible plight? Could the government have alleviated the destitution of the common people? Would the gentry have supported all actions the government might take? Why or why not?

## INTERNET ASSIGNMENT

**Keywords:** **Buddhist cave pictures**

***Tale of Genji***

Much of the art in the Buddhist caves of western China dates from about the time that the *Tale of Genji* was written. Use the keywords above to find websites on Buddhist caves and the *Tale of Genji*. You might want to consult the *History WIRED* image library on the Bulliet, *The Earth and Its Peoples* website (refer to the preface of this study guide for information on how to locate the Bulliet home page).

1. If you examine the artistic styles of the caves and the *Tale of Genji*, you will notice some similarities. What could account for those similarities?
2. What do these pieces of art demonstrate about the societies that created them?
3. How are the Buddhist caves of China and the *Tale of Genji* useful to modern scholars?

## INTERNET EXPLORATION

Poetry was always considered the perfect literary form in China, and during the Tang dynasty poetry reached its peak. One of the most beloved poets of the day was Li Bai (also known as Li Bo and Li Po). Use the keywords "Li Bai" to find some examples of his poetry. One site you may enjoy is http://www.chinapage.com/libai2n.html. Many of these sites have audio, Chinese characters, and English translations. What did Li Bai write about? Is his poetry still relevant today?

## MAP EXERCISE

On Outline Map 10.1 (provided below), mark the extent of these empires:

- Tang Empire
- Song Empire
- Liao Empire
- Uighur Empire
- Southern Song Empire
- Jin Empire
- Dai Viet Empire
- Champa Empire

Then plot the location of the following:

- Chang'an (Xi'an)
- Heian
- Sogdiana
- Ferghana
- Transoxiana
- Dunhuang
- Silla

## Outline Map 10.1

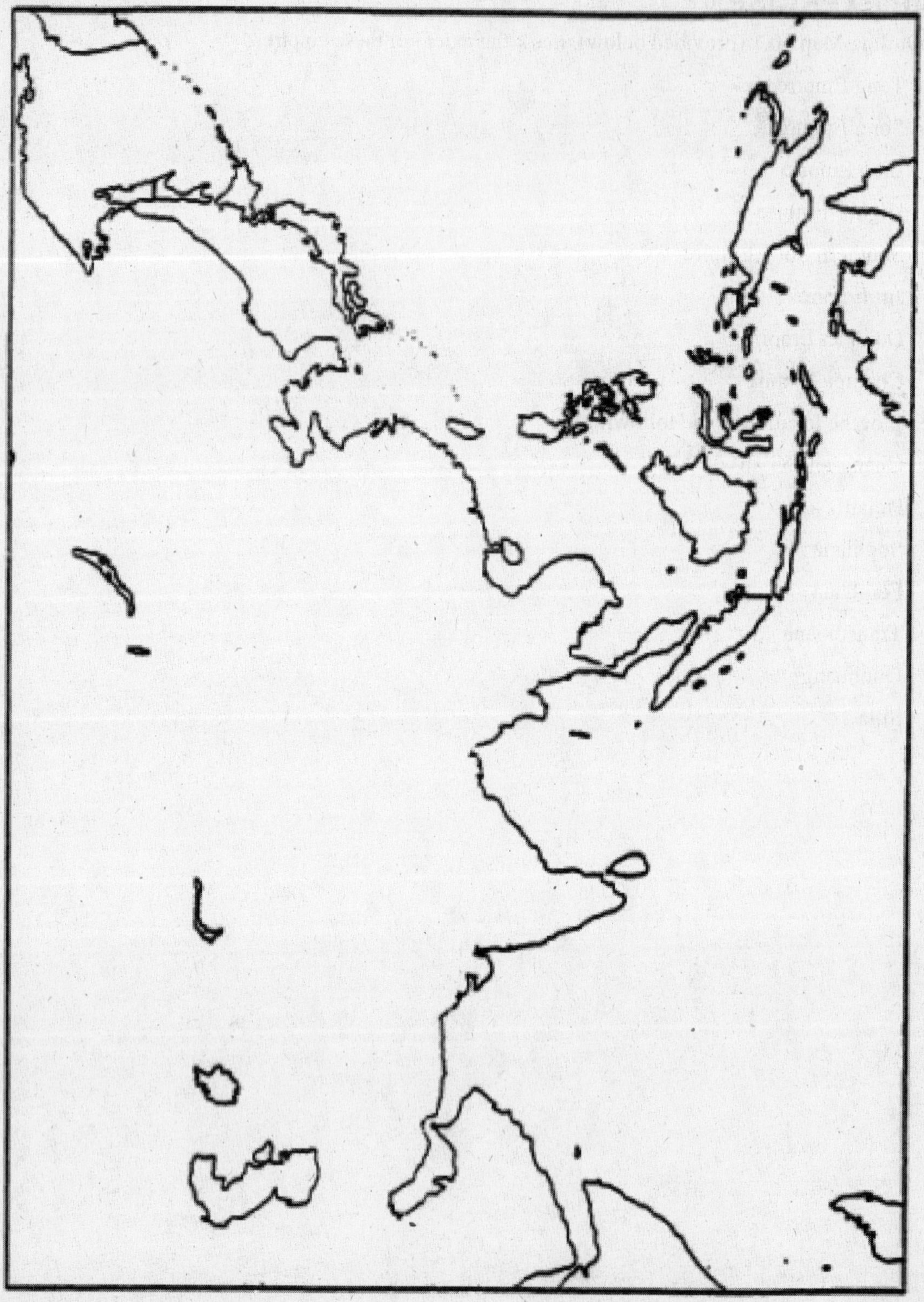

## FOCUS QUESTIONS

1. How did the role of cities develop during this period? What kinds of economic and cultural activity took place in cities?
2. How did Chinese culture influence surrounding areas outside China?
3. Was there an integrated network of economic activity by the year 1200 C.E.?
4. How significant were the artistic, scientific, and technological developments of the Tang and Song dynasties?
5. Why *didn't* China experience an industrial revolution before 1200 C.E.?

## ANSWERS TO MULTIPLE-CHOICE QUESTIONS

| | | |
|---|---|---|
| 1. | a | p. 273 |
| 2. | c | p. 268 |
| 3. | b | p. 272 |
| 4. | a | pp. 272–273 |
| 5. | e | p. 273 |
| 6. | e | p. 275 |
| 7. | b | p. 284 |
| 8. | d | p. 285 |
| 9. | a | p. 285 |
| 10. | d | p. 285 |
| 11. | e | p. 287 |
| 12. | c | p. 287 |
| 13. | a | p. 287 |
| 14. | c | pp. 287–288 |
| 15. | c | p. 281 |

CHAPTER 11

# Peoples and Civilizations of the Americas, 600–1500

## BEFORE YOU BEGIN

History is a science of interpreting incomplete evidence. Historians never have all the pieces to any puzzle, which is why the conclusions that historians draw using the evidence that does exist constantly evolve as new evidence is discovered or old evidence is reinterpreted. More than most other chapters, the Americas before 1500 C.E. are an example of how there is much more that we don't know than what we do. Large pieces of evidence remain a mystery either because they no longer exist or there is no known translation "key" that current scholars can understand.

You'll find numerous instances in this chapter where the authors refer to their interpretation by phrases like, "the evidence suggests . . ." or "one theory, which there is little evidence to support, is . . ." This is not a flaw or fault on the part of the authors; it is an inherent limitation in the discipline of historical scholarship. If you find the inexactitude disturbing, it just proves you're paying attention!

## LEARNING OBJECTIVES

After reading Chapter 11 and completing this study chapter, you should be able to:

- Explain how isolation from other continents shaped technological and social developments in the Americas.
- Explain how each region of the Americas differed geographically and how these differences influenced the development of the diverse cultures of the Americas.
- Describe the environmental challenges the peoples of the Americas faced and how they met those challenges.
- Explain how the cultural legacies of early cultures such as the Olmec and Chavín civilizations shaped the societies that followed them and why the cultural traditions of the Americas proved very durable.

## IDENTIFICATIONS

Define each term and explain why it is significant, including any important dates.

**maize**

______________________________________________

______________________________________________

**bloodletting rituals**

______________________________________________

______________________________________________

**Teotihuacan**

**chinampas**

**Maya**

**Toltecs**

**Aztecs**

**Tenochtitlan**

**tribute system**

**Huitzilopochtli**

**Anasazi**

**chiefdom**

**khipu**

**ayllu**

**mit'a**

**Moche**

**llamas and alpacas**

**Chimú**

**coca**

**Tiwanaku**

**Wari**

**Inca**

## MULTIPLE-CHOICE QUESTIONS

Read the entire question, including *all* the possible answers. Then choose the *one* answer that best fits the question.

1. Which of the following indicates that Teotihuacan probably used its military to expand its trade relations?
    a. The discovery of representations of soldiers in Teotihuacan dress in the Maya region of Guatemala
    b. Written accounts by the Maya and Moche
    c. Swords found in graves all over Mesoamerica
    d. Written accounts found in Teotihuacan
    e. Aztec codices
2. Typically, Maya military forces fought to secure
    a. trade goods and routes.
    b. captives rather than territory.
    c. territory rather than captives.
    d. territory and important religious sites.
    e. water ways.
3. Which of the following statements is *not* true about the postclassic period in Mesoamerica?
    a. The population decreased.
    b. Agricultural practices intensified.
    c. Many rulers increased the size of their armies.
    d. Rulers used new political institutions to facilitate their control of diverse peoples and regions.
    e. Warfare increased.
4. Which of the following is *not* true of the Toltecs?
    a. They created the first conquest state based largely on military power.
    b. Unlike earlier Mesoamerican societies, they never practiced human sacrifice.
    c. The Aztecs incorrectly believed that the Toltecs were the source of nearly all of the cultural achievements of the Mesoamerican world.
    d. Many Toltec public buildings were decorated with pictures of warriors.
    e. Their use of two chieftains eventually weakened the state.
5. What percentage of the Aztec capital's food requirement was met by tribute from conquered peoples?
    a. 10 percent
    b. 25 percent
    c. 40 percent
    d. 75 percent
    e. 100 percent
6. What did Huitzilopochtli need to sustain him in his daily struggle to bring the sun's warmth to the world?
    a. The blood of the king
    b. The worship of the people
    c. His mate Ixchel (the moon)
    d. A constant supply of human hearts
    e. Victories on the ball court

7. What is the most likely reason that the sites in Chaco Canyon were abandoned by the Anasazi?
   a. Warfare with the neighboring Hohokam, Sinagua, and Hopi
   b. Bubonic plague
   c. A long drought, which undermined the agricultural economy
   d. The migratory habits of the Anasazi, who moved several times a year
   e. Polluted water sources
8. Which of the following is *not* an attribute of North American chiefdoms?
   a. They contained a population of as many as 10,000 people.
   b. They were ruled by a chief, a hereditary leader with religious and secular duties.
   c. There were organized periodic rituals of feasts and gift giving.
   d. They engaged in long-distance trade, often with luxury goods.
   e. They managed large groups of people to build monumental architecture.
9. What is the most likely explanation for the Mississippian culture possessing the knowledge to grow maize, squash, and beans?
   a. The domestication of maize, squash, and beans originated in North America.
   b. They got it from Mesoamerican cultures.
   c. They developed it on their own.
   d. They learned it from the Anasazi.
   e. They learned it from contact with cultures living between them and Mesoamerica.
10. Unique environmental challenges led to especially distinctive highland and coastal cultures in
    a. the Andes.
    b. Mesoamerica.
    c. Chaco Canyon.
    d. the Ohio Valley.
    e. the land on both sides of the Gila River.
11. All scholars agree that the cultural center of Wari
    a. shared elements of the culture and technology of Tiwanaku.
    b. was a dependency of Tiwanaku.
    c. was a twin capital of Tiwanaku.
    d. was most closely related to the Nazca.
    e. None of these are correct. Scholars do not agree because there are many, as yet unproven, viable theories.
12. Which of the following has allowed scholars to trace Wari's expanding power?
    a. Tracing the spread of Wari pottery
    b. Wari and Tiwanakan written records
    c. Inca wall murals
    d. Excavation of royal burials
    e. Excavation of battle sites
13. The Inca civilization was originally based on
    a. control of religious institutions.
    b. military dominance.
    c. reciprocal gift giving and the redistribution of food and textiles.
    d. the control of jade, like the Olmec civilization.
    e. taking captives for sacrifice.

14. The Inca conquest of large populations in environmentally distinct regions permitted economic growth, but
    a. the population decreased.
    b. the population increased.
    c. it increased warfare with Mesoamerica.
    d. it caused eventual economic decline.
    e. it reduced equality among people.
15. Inca prosperity and military strength depended on
    a. human sacrifice.
    b. llamas and alpacas.
    c. khipus.
    d. agriculture.
    e. irrigation systems.
16. Which of the following is the best evidence that the post-classical cultures of North America and Mesoamerica were linked?
    a. Both cultures required military service of male citizens.
    b. The pyramids of Tikal resemble the terraced mound at Cahokia.
    c. Both the Anasazi and Maya religions centered around worshipping a sun god.
    d. Female priests were the norm in both regions.
    e. Both regions harvested corn (maize) as a staple food.

## ESSAY QUESTIONS

Make an outline for each question, listing the major points you want to discuss. Then write your practice essay, following your outline carefully and making sure that you do not skip any of your major points. At this time you will want to add the relevant dates and details that will make your essay persuasive and accurate.

### Change Over Time

1. What environmental conditions posed challenges for the peoples of the Americas? How did they cope with these challenges? Choose examples from three cultures.
2. Discuss cultural sharing, influence, and legacies among the peoples of the Americas. Use at least three examples.
3. Trace the rise and fall of two American cultures. What factors led to their initial success, how did they maintain power, and what led to their eventual demise?

### Compare and Contrast

1. Discuss the similarities that united the cultures of Mesoamerica. What divided them?
2. Compare and contrast the roles of women in Mayan, Aztec, and Incan societies.
3. Compare and contrast two North American cultures (excluding Mesoamerica). What were their political institutions, how did they provide food for their people, and what was their daily lifestyle?

### General Essay

1. What evidence do historians use to support their characterizations of American civilizations before 1500?

## COMPARISON CHARTS

Using information gathered from the text, fill in the blank areas of each chart with the relevant data pertaining to the regions and categories listed. (Not all blank areas will necessarily be equally complete.)

## Chart 11.1

### AMERICAN TECHNOLOGY

| | Agriculture/Migration/Flood Control | Mathematics/Astronomy | Art/Architecture/Urban Planning | Economics/Trade | Population Control | Politics |
|---|---|---|---|---|---|---|
| **Teotihuacan** | | | | | | |
| **Maya** | | | | | | |
| **Aztecs** | | | | | | |
| **Anasazi** | | | | | | |
| **Hopewell/Mississippian** | | | | | | |
| **Moche** | | | | | | |
| **Tiwanaku** | | | | | | |
| **Inca** | | | | | | |

## Chart 11.2

### THE MAYA, THE AZTECS, AND THE INCA

| | Region/Dates | Rise | Political System | Social Features | Internal and External Relations | Decline |
|---|---|---|---|---|---|---|
| **Maya** | | | | | | |
| **Aztecs** | | | | | | |
| **Inca** | | | | | | |

## DIVERSITY AND DOMINANCE

After reading "Diversity and Dominance: Burials as Historical Texts" in your text, answer the following additional questions.

1. What kinds of goods were buried with people?
2. If possession of these goods gave status to the living, do you think that burying those articles with the dead provided even more prestige?
3. Why don't threats and curses stop grave robbers?

## INTERNET ASSIGNMENT

**Keywords:** **Machu Picchu**

**Mesa Verde or cliff dwellings**

Both Machu Picchu and Mesa Verde were built by peoples belonging to sophisticated cultures. Use the above keywords to find websites about these structures. You might want to consult the *History WIRED* image library on the Bulliet, *The Earth and Its Peoples* website (refer to the preface of this study guide for information on how to locate the Bulliet home page).

1. Though the societies themselves appear to have been quite different, Machu Picchu and Mesa Verde were very similar. Why?
2. What may have motivated the builders to select these sites?
3. What are the two structures made of, and why?
4. What may account for their different preservation rates?

## INTERNET EXPLORATION

Today many people find the taste of chocolate divine, but did you know that, to the ancient Maya and Aztecs, chocolate *was* divine? Try the keywords "chocolate Maya and Aztec" to learn more about this sacred substance. Or try this specific website: http://www.mythinglinks.org/ip~cacao.html. Who brought chocolate to the ancient Mexicans? What ritual purposes were associated with chocolate?

## MAP EXERCISE

On Outline Map 11.1 (provided below), mark the extent of the following:

Maya civilization, 150 B.C.E.–900 C.E.

Aztec Empire, 1519 C.E.

Anasazi culture

Mound-building cultures

Moche state, 200–700 C.E.

Inca Empire, 1532 C.E.

Then plot the following:

Tenochtitlan

Tikal

Cuzco

Lake Titicaca

## Outline Map 11.1

## FOCUS QUESTIONS

1. What common social, cultural, economic, and political patterns existed among the Mayan, Aztec, and Incan civilizations?
2. What evidence do historians use to support their characterizations of American civilizations before 1500?
3. What opportunities and limitations existed before 1500 for elite women in American civilizations?

## ANSWERS TO MULTIPLE-CHOICE QUESTIONS

| | | |
|---|---|---|
| 1. | a | p. 295 |
| 2. | b | p. 296 |
| 3. | a | p. 298 |
| 4. | b | p. 299 |
| 5. | b | p. 301 |
| 6. | d | p. 301 |
| 7. | c | p. 304 |
| 8. | e | p. 305 |
| 9. | e | p. 305 |
| 10. | a | p. 305 |
| 11. | e | p. 310 |
| 12. | a | p. 310 |
| 13. | c | p. 310 |
| 14. | e | p. 311 |
| 15. | b | p. 311 |
| 16. | b | p. 305 |

CHAPTER 12

# Mongol Eurasia and Its Aftermath, 1200–1500

## BEFORE YOU BEGIN

The Mongols are a historical example that is prone to exaggeration and stereotyping. As you read this chapter, focus on how the Mongols adapt to the challenges and opportunities that existed in the later medieval period. While the Mongols certainly desired military conquest, their political, economic, technological, and religious impact on each conquered region was often unintentional. After the Mongols' influence waned, each Mongol-influenced region developed in a new direction, sometimes continuing but often rejecting Mongol practices.

## LEARNING OBJECTIVES

After reading Chapter 12 and completing this study chapter, you should be able to:

- Explain how the Mongols united under Genghis Khan, and discuss the factors particular to Central Asia that contributed to their rise.
- Discuss how the Mongols dominated large regions of Eurasia and what their long-term impact was, including facilitating the rise of nationalism; creating new, wealthy urban centers; and impoverishing the countryside.
- Explain how the peace imposed by the Mongols helped new ideas, goods, people, technology, and diseases travel the length of the Eurasian continent.
- Explain how the Mongols transformed China into a Mongol state, how the Chinese reacted to that transformation, and how later the Ming Empire addressed those changes wrought by the Mongols.
- Describe how Korea, Japan, and Vietnam developed during the Mongol period and in what ways Mongol occupation, or the threat of Mongol occupation, influenced their government policies and economic development.
- Explain how Mongol rule and legacy differed in western and eastern Eurasia.

## IDENTIFICATIONS

Define each term and explain why it is significant, including any important dates.

**Ögödei**

______________________________________________

______________________________________________

**Genghis Khan**

______________________________________________

______________________________________________

**Mongols**

**nomadism**

**bubonic plague**

**Il-khan**

**Golden Horde**

**Yuan Empire**

**Timur (Tamerlane)**

**tsar**

**Ottomans**

**lama**

**Zheng He**

**Beijing**

**kamikaze**

**Yongle**

**Khubilai Khan**

**Yi Kingdom**

**Ming Empire**

**Ashikaga Shogunate**

**cottage industries**

**Manchuria**

**Forbidden City**

**Yi Empire**

**movable type**

**Annam**

**Champa**

**steppe**

**Il-khan**

**Rashid al-Din**

**tax farming**

**Ibn Khaldun**

**"Arabic" numerals**

## MULTIPLE-CHOICE QUESTIONS

Read the entire question, including *all* the possible answers. Then choose the *one* answer that best fits the question.

1. The rise of Genghis Khan and the Mongols can be attributed
   a. solely to the charisma and military genius of Genghis Khan.
   b. to the incompetence of his competitors.
   c. at least partially to the long-term trends and pressures of Central Asia.
   d. to the lack of competition for resources in Central Asia.
   e. to unusual weather patterns in the twelfth century.

2. Which of the following best describes the religious atmosphere on the steppe?
   a. All steppe peoples followed the God Eternal Heaven exclusively.
   b. There was a mix of religious affiliations.
   c. Islam had quickly eroded all other influences.
   d. Buddhism still reigned supreme.
   e. Christianity had begun making significant inroads among the clans.
3. If attacked by the Mongols, what would be the best course of action?
   a. Negotiate.
   b. Meet out on the field where the Mongol cavalry was weak.
   c. Open the city gates to fight.
   d. Keep the gates closed, but don't surrender.
   e. Surrender.
4. What caused the "great pandemic" (bubonic plague, typhus, influenza, and smallpox) of 1347–1352?
   a. Peace and trade
   b. Mongol conquest
   c. European lack of sanitation
   d. Chinese lack of sanitation
   e. Massive migration from plague-infested Yunnan
5. Why did a diplomatic correspondence occur between Pope Nicholas IV and the Il-khan court?
   a. Pope Nicholas IV hoped to enlist the Il-khans in driving the Golden Horde from the Caucasus.
   b. Pope Nicholas IV needed to ransom the Christian residents of Jerusalem.
   c. The Il-khans were interested in converting to Christianity to distance themselves from Muslim Mongols.
   d. Physicians on both sides had been requesting diplomatic help to find a cure for the plague.
   e. European leaders believed that the Il-khans would help them to relieve Muslim pressure on the Crusader states.
6. To enhance their ability to control Russia, the Mongols
   a. granted privileges to the Orthodox Church.
   b. undermined local elites.
   c. converted to Christianity.
   d. promoted farmers to positions of power.
   e. had a partnership with the Russian elites.
7. Frederick II conspired with the Mamluks to give the illusion of having captured Jerusalem because he
   a. wanted the prestige of capturing the Holy Land so that he might become pope.
   b. was actually preparing for war against the Papal States.
   c. had lost the war and was paying tribute to the Mamluks.
   d. wanted to outflank the Mongols.
   e. was threatened with excommunication by the pope unless he helped in the military campaigns.
8. The Mongol armies in western Eurasia were made up mostly of
   a. ethnic Mongols.
   b. Uighur mercenaries.
   c. captured Christians.
   d. Mamluks.
   e. an international force.

9. What did a Confucian adviser talk Ögödei out of doing?
   a. Making Buddhism the official religion of China
   b. Defeating southern China
   c. Attacking Japan a third time
   d. Turning the rich agricultural land of northern China into pasture land
   e. Forming an alliance with the Jurchen
10. According to Mongol law, the status of people within their realms was based on
   a. individual merit.
   b. military expertise.
   c. where they or their ancestors were born.
   d. their educational level.
   e. a personal relationship with the Khan.
11. The Mongolian-influenced Chinese vernacular language is often called
   a. Uighur.
   b. Mandarin.
   c. Urdu.
   d. Hakka.
   e. Hmong.
12. Which of the following statements best characterizes the Mongol attitude toward farmers?
   a. They hated farming and so did nothing to help farmers.
   b. They saw agriculture only as a way to make money and so always exploited farmers.
   c. They were nomads and so didn't know about things like dams and dikes.
   d. They were enthusiastic about taking up farming themselves.
   e. They tried to protect farmers eventually, but it was too late.
13. The Ming Empire addressed the problem of hostile western Mongol control of the overland trade routes by
   a. ceasing trade.
   b. making war on the Mongols.
   c. sending Zheng He to establish connections by sea.
   d. sending Buddhist missionaries as diplomats to negotiate.
   e. bribing the Mongols.
14. Though the Ming dynasty is not known for its technological advancement, they did excel in
   a. metallurgy.
   b. porcelain production.
   c. shipbuilding.
   d. firearm production.
   e. printing techniques.
15. Koreans gained the secret formula for gunpowder
   a. by purchasing it from Chinese scientists.
   b. by purchasing it from Indian spies.
   c. from a Sogdian Buddhist monk.
   d. by subterfuge.
   e. by careful scientific research.
16. What saved the Japanese from certain defeat by the Mongols?
   a. Poor Mongol military tactics
   b. Superior Japanese military tactics
   c. The plague
   d. Advance warning from Korea
   e. The wind

17. From the traditional Chinese point of view, the most objectionable Mongol practice of the Yuan Dynasty was that
    a. Mongol men often married elite Chinese women, depriving Chinese men of favorable marriage prospects.
    b. the Chinese were not allowed to learn the Mongol language, leaving the Chinese largely illiterate.
    c. the Mongols held traditional Confucian scholars in low esteem, restricting most high-ranking government offices to foreigners loyal only to the Mongols.
    d. the Mongols closed the Grand Canal to Chinese merchants, which severely damaged the economy.
    e. the Mongols considered merchants and physicians to be a higher social class than traditional Chinese culture did.

# ESSAY QUESTIONS

Make an outline for each question, listing the major points you want to discuss. Then write your practice essay, following your outline carefully and making sure that you do not skip any of your major points. At this time, you will want to add the relevant dates and details that will make your essay persuasive and accurate.

## Change Over Time

1. Discuss the legacy of the Mongols in western and eastern Eurasia. How did they affect the political, economic, religious, and social systems of the peoples they conquered and the peoples they attempted to conquer?

2. Discuss Mongol military technology and governmental techniques. How did the combination of the two bring about the subjugation of most of Eurasia, the control of great masses of people, and the impoverishment of much of the countryside?

3. How did the art, science, and intellectual developments of Islamic Eurasia affect Europe? Use specific examples of each.

4. Why did the Yongle emperor send Zheng He on his voyages of exploration, what did they accomplish, and why were they ended?

## Compare and Contrast

1. Compare and contrast the lifestyles of nomadic and sedentary peoples. How did each earn their livelihood, what was their daily life like, and how did they relate to outside groups?

# COMPARISON CHARTS

Using information gathered from the text, fill in the blank areas of each chart with the relevant data pertaining to the regions and categories listed. (Not all blank areas will necessarily be equally complete.)

Chart 12.1

## NOMADIC VERSUS SEDENTARY LIFESTYLES

| | Geography | Livelihood | Diet | Political Structure | Social Structure | Technology | Population Density | Examples of Peoples |
|---|---|---|---|---|---|---|---|---|
| Nomads | | | | | | | | |
| Settled Peoples | | | | | | | | |

Chart 12.2

MONGOL INFLUENCE ON WESTERN VERSUS EASTERN EURASIA

| | Native Reaction | Utilization of Technology | Economy and Trade | Religion | Society | Internal Threats | External Threats |
|---|---|---|---|---|---|---|---|
| Western Eurasia | | | | | | | |
| Eastern Eurasia | | | | | | | |

## DIVERSITY AND DOMINANCE

After reading "Diversity and Dominance: Mongol Politics, Mongol Women" in your text, answer the following additional questions.

1. How are male "betrayers" and female "betrayers" treated differently in the selection? Why?
2. Though women are shown to have influence, they still could not hold the title of khan. Why do you think that might be?

## INTERNET ASSIGNMENT

**Keywords:** **Beijing, the Forbidden City**

**Zen gardens**

Architecture is one way that a society expresses itself, and therefore much can be learned about societies from studying art and architecture. Use the above keywords to find websites about the Forbidden City in China and Japanese Zen gardens. You might want to consult the *History WIRED* image library at the Bulliet, *The Earth and Its Peoples* website (refer to the preface of this study guide for information on how to locate the Bulliet home page).

1. When you view pictures of the Forbidden City in China, what kind of culture do you think of?
2. When you look at Japanese Zen gardens, what kind of outlook do you think the people who created them had?
3. Can you find any common ground between the Forbidden City and the Zen gardens?

## INTERNET EXPLORATION

Modern-day Mongolians have inherited a rich tradition of "world" domination from their Mongol ancestors. Use the keywords "Genghis Khan," "virtual Mongolia," and "yurt" to compare the life of today's Mongols to the time of the Great Khans. What influence has the environment had on the life of the peoples of the steppe?

## MAP EXERCISE

On Outline Map 12.1, trace the route of Marco Polo and of the Mongol raids. Then mark the extent of the domain of the following:

Great Khan

Khanate of the Golden Horde

Khanate of Jagadai

Il-khans

On Outline Map 12.2, trace Zheng He's voyages and mark the extent of the Ming Empire. Then plot these cities:

Beijing

Nanjing

Shangdu

## Outline Map 12.1

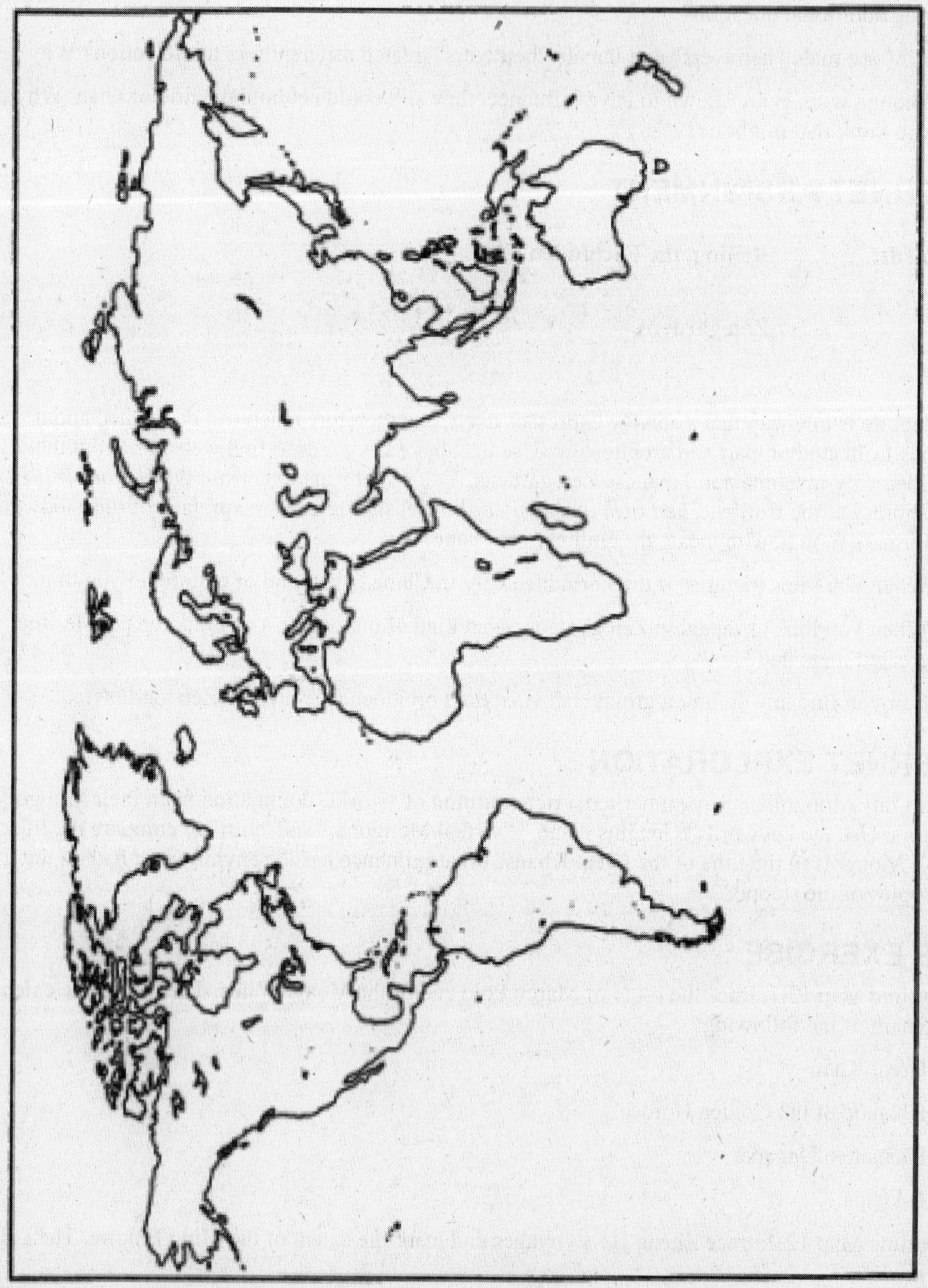

## FOCUS QUESTIONS

1. How did the Mongols directly impact the areas they conquered, as well as indirectly impact the surrounding areas?
2. What were the social, economic, political, and religious effects of the bubonic plague?
3. How did the Mongols affect the Eurasian trade networks?

## ANSWERS TO MULTIPLE-CHOICE QUESTIONS

1. c p. 324
2. b p. 340
3. e p. 330
4. a p. 331
5. a p. 331
6. a p. 335
7. e p. 337
8. e p. 337
9. d p. 338
10. c p. 339
11. b p. 339
12. e p. 339
13. c p. 338
14. b p. 345
15. d p. 346
16. e p. 347
17. c p. 339

# CHAPTER 13

# Tropical Africa and Asia, 1200–1500

## BEFORE YOU BEGIN

The most important geographical area in this chapter isn't land at all. The Indian Ocean basin became more interconnected and formed the most developed, sophisticated trade region on earth before 1500 C.E. Trade was facilitated by an intricate combination of geological, ecological, and human factors. Islam played a large role in this system. Pay careful attention to the ways that Islam both affected and was affected by the societies to which it spread.

## LEARNING OBJECTIVES

After reading Chapter 13 and completing this study chapter, you should be able to:

- Discuss how the peoples of the tropics adapted to their environments, what specific techniques or innovations helped them survive, and how certain features of Africa and South Asia united the two regions.
- Describe the process by which trade was carried out on the Indian Ocean, who participated, what kind of vessels were used, what goods were exchanged, and who benefited from the system.
- Explain how Islam affected different societies in regard to economics, education, status of women, and architecture.
- Explain how the similarities and differences among the regions of Africa, the Middle East, India, and Southeast Asia affected their political, economic, and social systems, and how the adoption of Islam influenced them differently depending on their circumstances.

## IDENTIFICATIONS

Define each term and explain why it is significant, including any important dates.

**tropics**

______________________________________________

______________________________________________

**Ibn Battuta**

______________________________________________

______________________________________________

**monsoon**

______________________________________________

______________________________________________

**Delhi Sultanate**

**farming**

**gold**

**Mali**

**Delhi**

**Mansa Musa**

**Gujarat**

**Raziya**

**dhow**

**junks**

**Swahili Coast**

**Great Zimbabwe**

**Aden**

**Malacca**

**Urdu**

**Timbuktu**

**slaves**

## MULTIPLE-CHOICE QUESTIONS

Read the entire question, including *all* the possible answers. Then choose the *one* answer that best fits the question.

1. Which of the following did *not* link the peoples of Africa and southern Asia?
   a. Islam
   b. Language
   c. Trade
   d. The environment
   e. Legal codes
2. The dominant way of life for most tropical peoples between 1200 and 1500 was
   a. food gathering.
   b. animal husbandry.
   c. agriculture.
   d. trade and commerce.
   e. manufacture.
3. Why did India have to import gold for jewelry and temple decoration from 1200 to 1500?
   a. It had no gold of its own.
   b. It had exhausted its own gold resources.
   c. So many temples were built that gold mining in India could not keep up with the pace.
   d. It had trade agreements with Africa and Southeast Asia that required these imports in order to correct a trade imbalance.
   e. The growing Shiva sect demanded more and more gold for its offerings.

4. The role of force in spreading Islam south of the Sahara was
   a. limited.
   b. considerable.
   c. encouraged by the Quran.
   d. encouraged by the ulama.
   e. combined with trade.
5. Which of the following was *not* a factor in the decline of the Delhi Sultanate?
   a. Rivalries within the Muslim elite
   b. The rulers depended more on terror than on toleration
   c. The discontent of the Hindus
   d. A tendency to pillage and levy high taxes to support the elite
   e. Intermarriage between Hindus and Muslims
6. How did the collapse of the Mongol Empire in the fourteenth century affect trade?
   a. The overland trade route grew in importance.
   b. The Indian Ocean trade route grew in importance.
   c. All trade between western and eastern Eurasia stopped.
   d. The Delhi Sultanate collapsed.
   e. The collapse of the Mongol Empire did not affect Eurasian trade.
7. The trade on the Indian Ocean was
   a. competitive and divisive.
   b. run by imperial decree.
   c. decentralized and cooperative.
   d. never very important to the economy of the area.
   e. plagued by warfare.
8. Why did the Chinese send a fleet to the Strait of Malacca in 1407?
   a. To take control of the region from the Kingdom of Siam
   b. To take control of the region from the Java-based kingdom of Majapahit
   c. To arrest a band of Chinese pirates who controlled the city of Palembang
   d. To establish a Chinese outpost there to dominate trade in the region
   e. To colonize Southeast Asia
9. Which of the following words is *not* Arabic in origin?
   a. Sahara
   b. Sudan
   c. Silk
   d. Swahili
   e. Monsoon
10. Which of the following groups was most instrumental in the spread of Islam?
    a. Soldiers
    b. Monarchs
    c. Merchants
    d. Peasants
    e. Monks
11. Which of the following was *least* responsible for the spread of Islam?
    a. Imperial decree
    b. Marriage
    c. Upheavals that helped to wipe out competing religions
    d. Muslim domination of trade and markets
    e. The fact that servants in Muslim households were required to convert to Islam

12. The rising prosperity of the elites was accompanied by
    a. peace.
    b. an increase in slavery.
    c. a decrease in religious fervor.
    d. inflation.
    e. the poor getting poorer.
13. Why, according to historians, has the art of brewing received more attention than other "female" arts, such as culinary skills?
    a. Brewing was also a way to make extra money.
    b. Brewing took more skill than cooking.
    c. Mildly alcoholic beverages can be nutritious.
    d. Men tended to be the principal consumers of beer.
    e. Muslims are not allowed to consume alcohol, so its consumption is a sin.
14. Which of the following is *not* characteristic of a dhow?
    a. Lateen sails
    b. Mounted cannon
    c. Sewn hull
    d. A rudder
    e. Planks made of teak
15. Which of the following best describes the relationship between Islam and the political leadership in Mali and the Delhi Sultanate?
    a. Mali rulers practiced a heretical brand of Islam, while the Delhi Sultanate was led by Shi'ite rulers.
    b. While Islam was the religion of the ruling class, it was actually the religion of a minority of the population in both Mali and the Delhi Sultanate.
    c. Mansa Musa and Timur (Tamerlane) were both friends of Ibn Battuta and sponsored his travels throughout the Islamic world.
    d. Both the Mali and Delhi Sultanate rulers were descended from the Mongol Il-Khan Hülegü.
    e. Islam came to Mali peacefully before the Mali Empire existed, while in India Islam usually spread through military conquest.

## ESSAY QUESTIONS

Make an outline for each question, listing the major points you want to discuss. Then write your practice essay, following your outline carefully and making sure that you do not skip any of your major points. At this time, you will want to add the relevant dates and details that will make your essay persuasive and accurate.

### Change Over Time

1. How did the peoples of the tropics adapt to their environments? What specific techniques or innovations helped them survive?

2. Describe the systems of extensive and intensive agriculture. What environmental, technological, and social factors influenced people to choose one system over the other? What advantages and disadvantages did each have?

3. Describe the process by which trade was conducted on the Indian Ocean. Who participated, what kinds of vessels were used, what goods were exchanged, and who benefited from the system?

4. Discuss how Islam affected economics, education, the status of women, and architecture in the different societies it encountered.

5. How did Islam change as it spread throughout the Indian Ocean basin and into sub-Saharan Africa?

## Compare and Contrast

1. Compare sub-Saharan Africa's and Europe's interaction with the Islamic world (see Chapter 14).

## General Essay

1. The writings of Ibn Battuta have long been valued by historians for their perception, veracity, and appeal. Give some examples of his work and discuss them. Can you think of any disadvantages to using his writing?
2. Was Islam more of a uniting or dividing force in the Indian Ocean trading basin before 1500?

## COMPARISON CHARTS

Using information gathered from the text, fill in the blank areas of each chart with the relevant data pertaining to the regions and categories listed. (Not all blank areas will necessarily be equally complete.)

Chart 13.1

TWO MUSLIM EMPIRES

| | Dates | Regions | Founding | Government System | Economy and Trade | Society | Technology | Internal Threats | External Threats | Role of Islam | Decline |
|---|---|---|---|---|---|---|---|---|---|---|---|
| Mali | | | | | | | | | | | |
| Delhi | | | | | | | | | | | |

Chart 13.2

## INDIAN OCEAN TRADE NETWORK

| | Dates | Trading Partners | Trade Goods | Technology | Resources | Society | Cities/Urban Planning | Religion | Decline |
|---|---|---|---|---|---|---|---|---|---|
| **Swahili Coast and Zimbabwe** | | | | | | | | | |
| **Arabia: Aden and the Red Sea** | | | | | | | | | |
| **India: Gujarat and the Malabar Coast** | | | | | | | | | |
| **Southeast Asia: The rise of Malacca** | | | | | | | | | |

## DIVERSITY AND DOMINANCE

After reading "Diversity and Dominance: Personal Styles of Rule in India and Mali" in your text, answer the following additional questions.

1. Can you find evidence of Ibn Battuta's views and opinions in these writings?
2. Which ruler might Ibn Battuta identify with and why?

## INTERNET ASSIGNMENT

**Keywords:** **Great Zimbabwe**

**Dhow building** or **Arab dhows**

The culture around the Indian Ocean Trading Basin was quite diverse. Use the above keywords to find websites about the ruins at Great Zimbabwe and dhow sailing vessels. You might want to consult the *History WIRED* image library on the Bulliet, *The Earth and Its Peoples* website (refer to the preface of this study guide for information on how to locate the Bulliet home page).

1. How do the ruins at Great Zimbabwe and the design of the dhow symbolize the cultures of the Indian Ocean peoples?
2. What links the city of Great Zimbabwe and the dhow sailing vessels?

## INTERNET EXPLORATION

Ibn Battuta was a great chronicler of the Muslim world. He traveled far and wide, and kept an interesting record of his experiences. What was life like on the road? What kinds of places did Ibn Battuta find interesting and how did he view the people he encountered? Do his records have any evidence of how people received him?

## MAP EXERCISES

On Outline Map 13.1, mark the wind direction of the two monsoon seasons.

On Outline Map 13.2, mark the following:

- Swahili Coast
- Great Zimbabwe
- Mali
- Aden
- Timbuktu
- Zeila

Then trace the Portuguese routes of exploration and the Muslim trade routes.

On Outline Map 13.3, shade in the extent of the Delhi Sultanate in 1236, the Delhi Sultanate in 1335, and the Delhi Sultanate lands lost in 1335.

On Outline Map 13.4, trace Ibn Battuta's routes. Then mark the extent of these areas:

- Majapahit Empire
- The Islamic world in 850
- Lands reconquered by Christian kingdoms by 1000
- The Islamic world in 1500

Also plot the following:

- Malacca
- Java
- Delhi
- Gujarat

## Outline Map 13.1

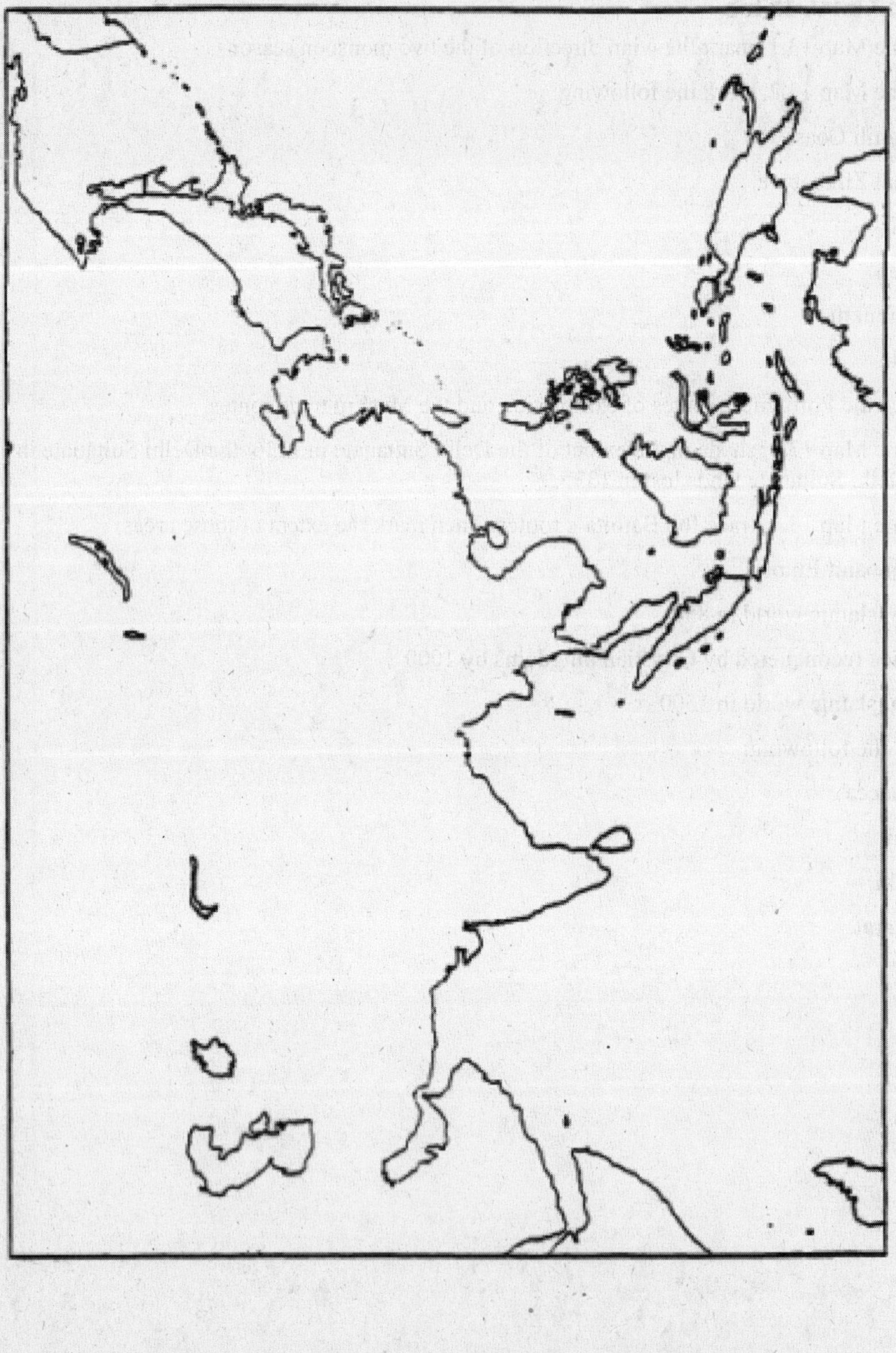

## Outline Map 13.2

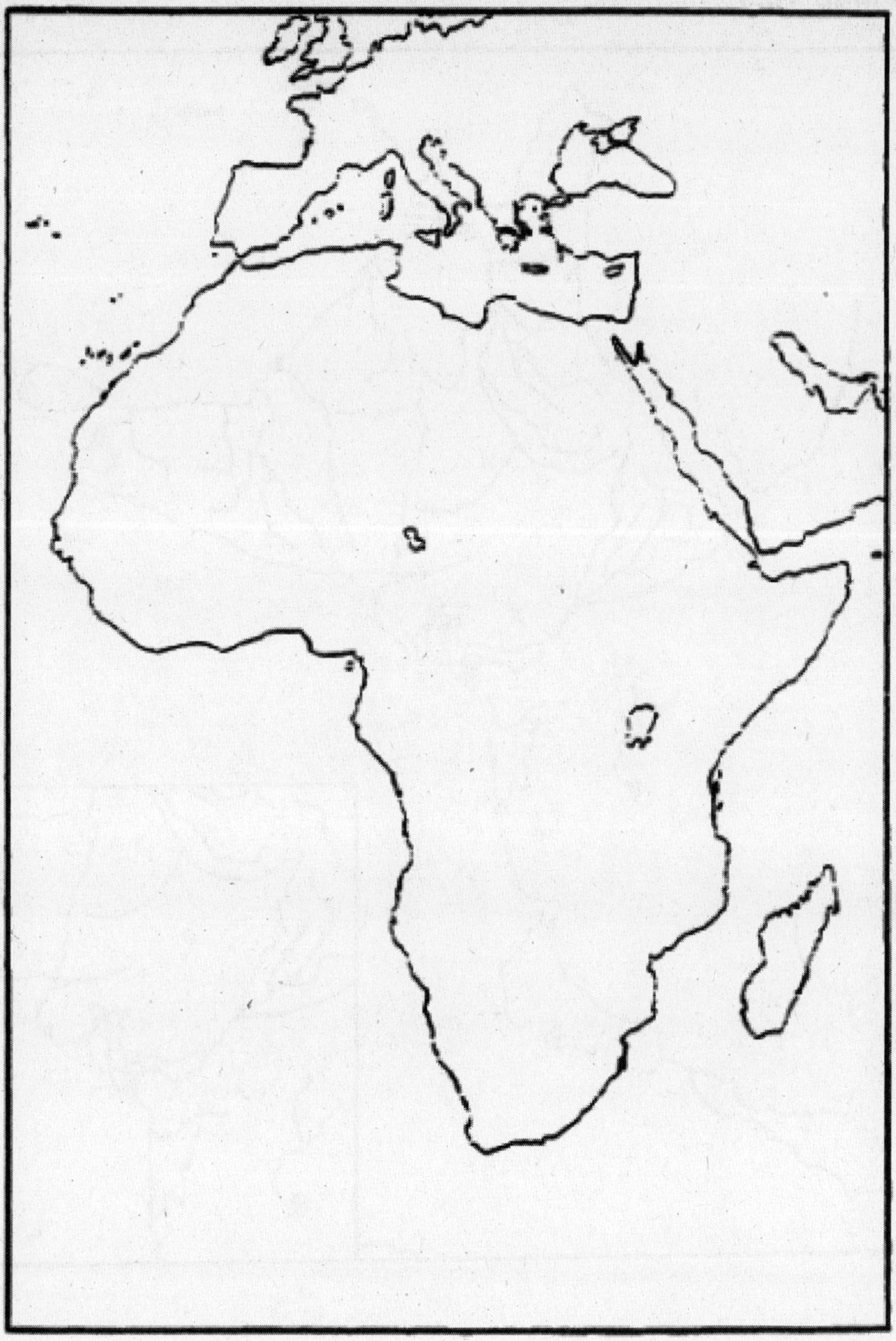

## Outline Map 13.3

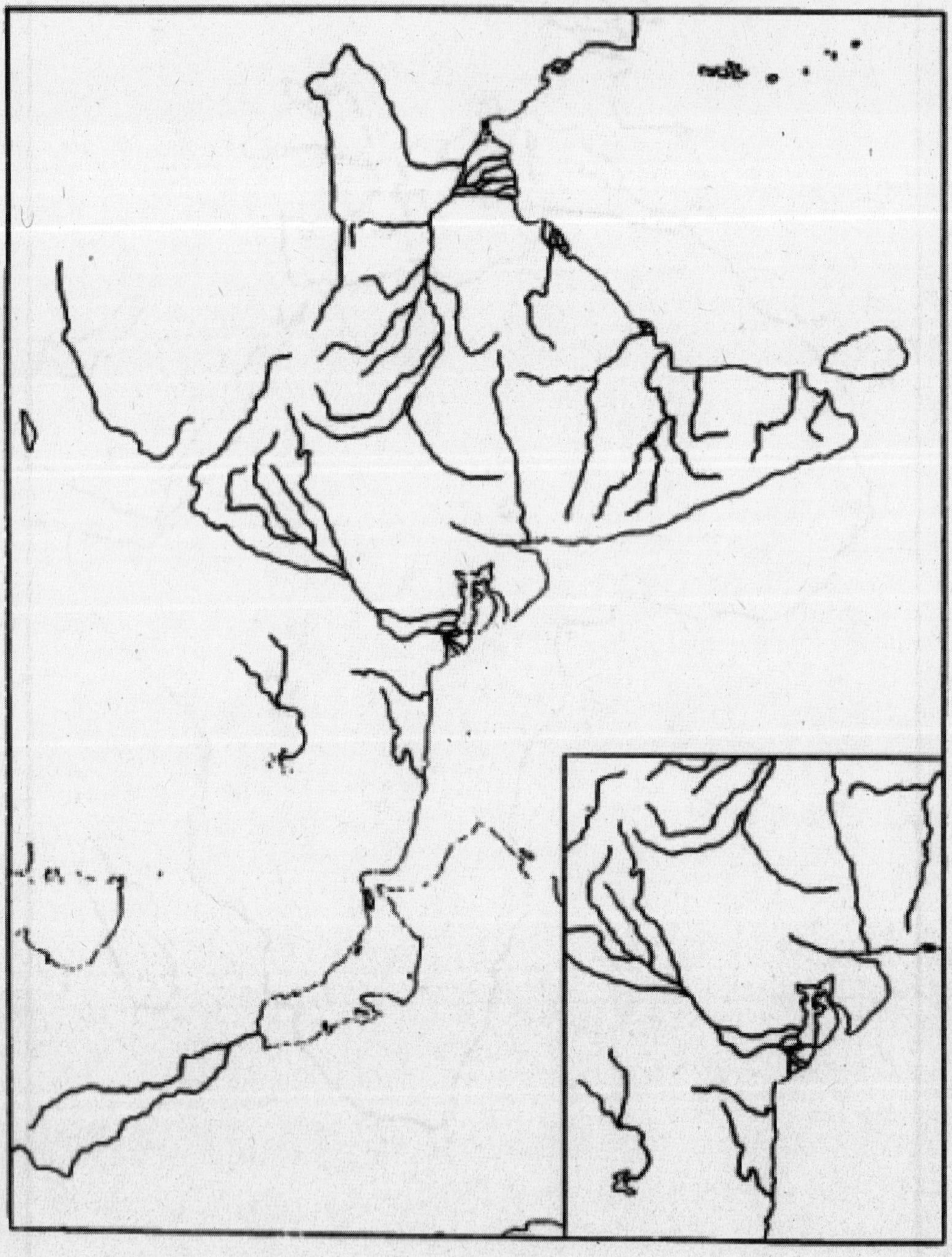

## Outline Map 13.4

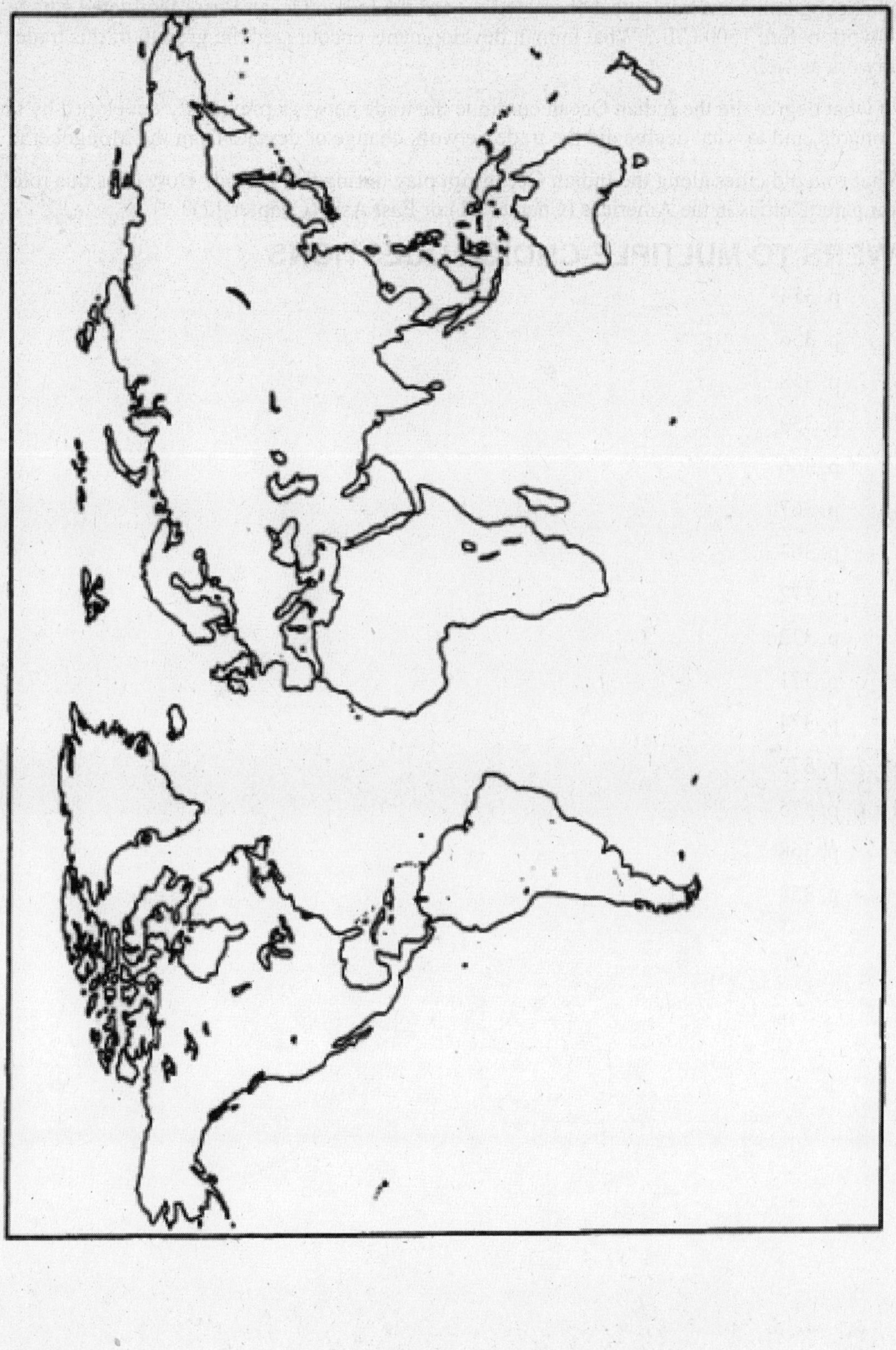

## FOCUS QUESTIONS

1. What geographic and ecological characteristics of the Indian Ocean Basin facilitated a trade network before 1500 C.E.? What human developments encouraged the growth of this trade network as well?
2. To what degree did the Indian Ocean continue the trade network previously developed by the Mongols, and to what degree did the trade network change or deviate from the Mongol era?
3. What role did cities along the Indian Ocean rim play during this period? How does this role compare to cities in the Americas (Chapter 11) or East Asia (Chapter 12)?

## ANSWERS TO MULTIPLE-CHOICE QUESTIONS

1. b p. 354
2. c p. 356
3. b p. 358
4. a p. 359
5. e p. 366
6. b p. 367
7. c p. 367
8. c p. 372
9. c p. 372
10. c p. 371
11. a p. 374
12. b p. 372
13. d p. 375
14. b p. 368
15. e p. 358

CHAPTER 14

# The Latin West, 1200–1500

## BEFORE YOU BEGIN

Chapters 1–7 address world history up to the year 600 C.E. (called "Foundations" in AP World History). Chapters 8–14 focus on the second period/era, from 600 to 1500 C.E.[1] Obviously there are major developments that distinguish 600–1500 from the earlier period, but have you noticed any subtle changes in the way the textbook organizes the information in this period? Each chapter in the Foundations period focuses on political and/or geographic entities (e.g., Roman Empire and Han China), while most of Chapters 8–14 emphasize a region's *cultural influence* more than its *political rule*. This doesn't mean the political entities aren't important, but understanding a cultural identity helps one more accurately understand this era more than focusing solely on a political boundary. Before you begin the post-1500 period, ask yourself this question: How would I understand 600–1500 C.E. differently if I studied it by political rather than by cultural boundaries?

This chapter is a great example of Change Over Time. Compare the Latin West in 1200 to1500 C.E. by almost any characteristic and you'll see that the region as a whole has slowly morphed into a new form. Good students will be able to *describe* the step-by-step *process* of this transformation, noting the starting point as well as the final result, while excellent students will *analyze* the historical *reasons* for the metamorphosis and support their interpretation of those reasons with historical facts.

## LEARNING OBJECTIVES

After reading Chapter 14 and completing this study chapter, you should be able to:

- Explain how Latin Europe changed during the Late Middle Ages, and how those changes affected the growth of cities, trade, the economy, the status of women, and the use of the environment.
- Explain how Latin Europe began its evolution from a feudal system to a centralized monarchy, and what was involved in this process.
- Discuss how the Renaissance grew out of the intellectual milieu of the Middle Ages; how Greco-Roman art and writings preserved by Italy, Byzantium, and the Islamic world influenced it; and in what ways Muslim and Chinese science contributed to the ideas of the Renaissance.
- Discuss how the many technological, economic, and social innovations of the Late Middle Ages and the Renaissance in Latin Europe were to change the face of Europe and the world.

---

[1] AP World History officially divides the chronological eras of study as follows: 8000 B.C.E.–600 C.E.; 600–1450 C.E.; 1450–1750; 1750–1914; and 1914–present. The textbook ends this era at 1500 instead of 1450 C.E. This is a small difference between the organizational structure of the textbook and the course. As you study key historical events and trends, keep in mind that a few interpretations of historical developments may change depending on whether one views them in the context of 600–1450/1500, or 1450/1500–1750, such as the Ottoman conquest of Byzantium (1453) or Columbus's discovery of the Americas (1492).

## IDENTIFICATIONS

Define each term and explain why it is significant, including any important dates.

**Latin West**

**serfs**

**three-field system**

**Black Death**

**water wheel**

**mills**

**Hanseatic League**

**European Jews**

**guild**

**Gothic cathedrals**

**Renaissance (European)**

**universities**

**scholasticism**

**humanists (Renaissance)**

**printing press**

**Great Western Schism**

**Hundred Years War**

**new monarchies**

**reconquest of Iberia**

**Magna Carta**

**clocks**

## MULTIPLE-CHOICE QUESTIONS

Read the entire question, including *all* the possible answers. Then choose the *one* answer that best fits the question.

1. Which of the following best explains Europe's population increase by 1300?
   a. The economy was reviving.
   b. Temperatures were warmer than usual.
   c. There were no severe epidemics.
   d. The new three-field system was introduced.
   e. There is no best answer because historians just do not know for certain.
2. What most eased population pressure in Europe in the fourteenth century?
   a. Improved agricultural techniques
   b. Deaths caused by the Mongol invasions
   c. Migration to the Holy Land
   d. The Black Death
   e. Birth control
3. All of the following aided the Latin West's economic transformation from 1200 to 1500 C.E. *except*
   a. borrowing paper making technology from the Chinese.
   b. the manufacturing of luxury goods previously available only from Muslim merchants.
   c. fierce competition among Italian city-states for profitable trade routes with the Middle East.
   d. strict control of the money supply by the Roman Catholic officials.
   e. the growth of humanist ideas and universities.
4. Most urban growth in the Latin West after 1200 stemmed from
   a. an influx of gold from Africa.
   b. the continuing growth of trade and manufacturing.
   c. the clearing of new farmland.
   d. improvements in breeding techniques of farm animals.
   e. improvements in medicine.
5. The Fourth Crusade was
   a. an attempt by Venetians to cripple Constantinople in order to gain better access to eastern trade.
   b. a last, futile attempt to hold on to the Holy Land.
   c. an attempt by the Holy Roman Emperor to take over the Byzantine Empire.
   d. not approved by the pope.
   e. deemed too costly and so was never executed.
6. Which of the following was the first to use heavy machinery in the production of paper?
   a. The Chinese
   b. The Muslims
   c. The Europeans
   d. The Africans
   e. The Koreans

7. Latin European cities were able to adapt more quickly to changing market conditions than cities in China and the Islamic world because they were
   a. autonomous.
   b. under direct imperial control.
   c. controlled by the nobles.
   d. more numerous.
   e. lacking in leadership.

8. Which of the following was *not* an attribute of Gothic architecture?
   a. Round arches
   b. External or "flying" buttresses
   c. Thin stone columns below arches
   d. Great height
   e. Giant stained-glass windows

9. Modern historians see the Renaissance as
   a. a sudden break from the Dark Ages.
   b. high noon of a day that had been dawning for centuries.
   c. caused solely by the rediscovery of classical texts.
   d. caused solely by Muslim influence.
   e. caused by reforms in the Catholic Church.

10. The Great Western Schism was finally resolved
    a. by the Protestant Reformation.
    b. by returning the pope to Rome, but Catholicism's political power was broken.
    c. by the Fourth Crusade against Constantinople.
    d. when the pope in Avignon died.
    e. by the Council of Trent.

11. Which of the following did *not* allow the new monarchs (fifteenth century) to undermine noble resistance to their growing power?
    a. Smaller mobile cannon
    b. Powerful handheld firearms
    c. Bowmen and pikemen
    d. Additional taxes levied in times of war
    e. The Great Western Schism

12. Which of the following did Ferdinand of Aragon and Isabella of Castile *not* gain in their takeover of Granada?
    a. A large population of Jewish bankers and merchants to help them finance Columbus's voyages
    b. Irrigated fields capable of producing an abundance of food
    c. Rich cities of glittering Moorish architecture
    d. Ports offering access to the Mediterranean and the South Atlantic
    e. A new crusade against Muslims

## ESSAY QUESTIONS

Make an outline for each question, listing the major points you want to discuss. Then write your practice essay, following your outline carefully and making sure that you do not skip any of your major points. At this time, you will want to add the relevant dates and details that will make your essay persuasive and accurate.

## Change Over Time

1. Discuss the ecological effects of industry in medieval Europe.
2. Trace the growth of European industry, technology, and trade in the Middle Ages through the development of the textile industry.
3. Discuss the role of guilds, and explain how they functioned on a social, political, and economic level.
4. How did Europe benefit from cultural borrowing? From whom did they borrow and what was borrowed?
5. Discuss the relationship among monarchs, nobles, and the church during the reigns of the new monarchs. Was this relationship different from that in feudal times? Why or why not?
6. How did the major economic, social, and political elements of Europe change from 1200 to 1500 C.E.?

## Compare and Contrast

1. Compare Japanese and European feudalism (see Chapter 12).
2. Compare the opportunities and limitations that elite women experienced before 1500 C.E. in *two* of the following regions: Europe, Middle East, East Asia (see Chapters 12 and 13).
3. Compare sub-Saharan Africa's and Europe's interaction with the Islamic world (see Chapter 13).

# COMPARISON CHARTS

Using information gathered from the text, fill in the blank areas of each chart with the relevant data pertaining to the regions and categories listed. (Not all blank areas will necessarily be equally complete.)

## Chart 14.1

### EUROPE'S FIRST INDUSTRIAL REVOLUTION: INDIGENOUS AND BORROWED ELEMENTS

| | Agriculture | Transporta-tion and Navigation | Military | Mechanical Energy | Metallurgy and Mining | Navigation | Textiles | Paper and Printing | Math and Physics | Medicine | Education |
|---|---|---|---|---|---|---|---|---|---|---|---|
| Latin Europe: Late Middle Ages | | | | | | | | | | | |
| Latin Europe: Renaissance | | | | | | | | | | | |
| Influence from Byzantium | | | | | | | | | | | |
| Influence from Muslims | | | | | | | | | | | |
| Influence from China | | | | | | | | | | | |

Chart 14.2

## THE BLACK DEATH IN EUROPE

| | Population | Symptoms and Life Expectancy | Psychological Effects | Resources | Economy and Labor | Government Response | Social Structure | Social Unrest |
|---|---|---|---|---|---|---|---|---|
| **Before the Plague** | | | | | | | | |
| **Plague Years** | | | | | | | | |
| **Recovery** | | | | | | | | |

## DIVERSITY AND DOMINANCE

After reading "Diversity and Dominance: Persecution and Protection of the Jews, 1272–1349" in your text, answer the following additional questions.

1. Jews died during the plague as well; how do you suppose Christians explained this?
2. Do you think that some Christians were confused by the pope's protection of the Jews in Avignon? How might they have explained his protection of the Jews?
3. What do you think of the final statement that the Jews would not have been burned had they not been rich?

## INTERNET ASSIGNMENT

**Keywords:** **Gothic cathedral**

***School of Athens***

While much of life for most people remained the same during the transition from the Middle Ages to the Renaissance, the world of ideas began to shift. Use the above keywords to find websites about Gothic cathedrals and Raphael's painting *School of Athens, Raphael*. You might want to consult the *History WIRED* image library on the Bulliet, *The Earth and Its Peoples* website (refer to the preface of this study guide for information on how to locate the Bulliet home page).

1. How are Gothic cathedrals representative of the Late Middle Ages?
2. How does Raphael's painting *School of Athens* represent the new ideas of the Renaissance?
3. Can you find any similarities between the two works of art?

## INTERNET EXPLORATION

When you think of the European Middle Ages, you probably think of King Arthur. Many scholars, however, think he may have lived as early as the fifth century C.E. (during the fall of the western Roman Empire). Many scholars even think that Arthur was legendary. The reason we associate him with Medieval Europe is that stories about him were quite popular then. Use the keywords "King Arthur Legend" to find many fascinating websites and many different theories about Arthur. What evidence supports the theory that Arthur was an actual figure? Why might he be legendary? What made him so appealing to Europeans of the Middle Ages? What makes him so fascinating to us today?

## MAP EXERCISE

On Outline Map 14.1, shade in the course of the Black Death during the following years, using different colors:

1347

1348

1349

1350

After 1350

## Outline Map 14.1

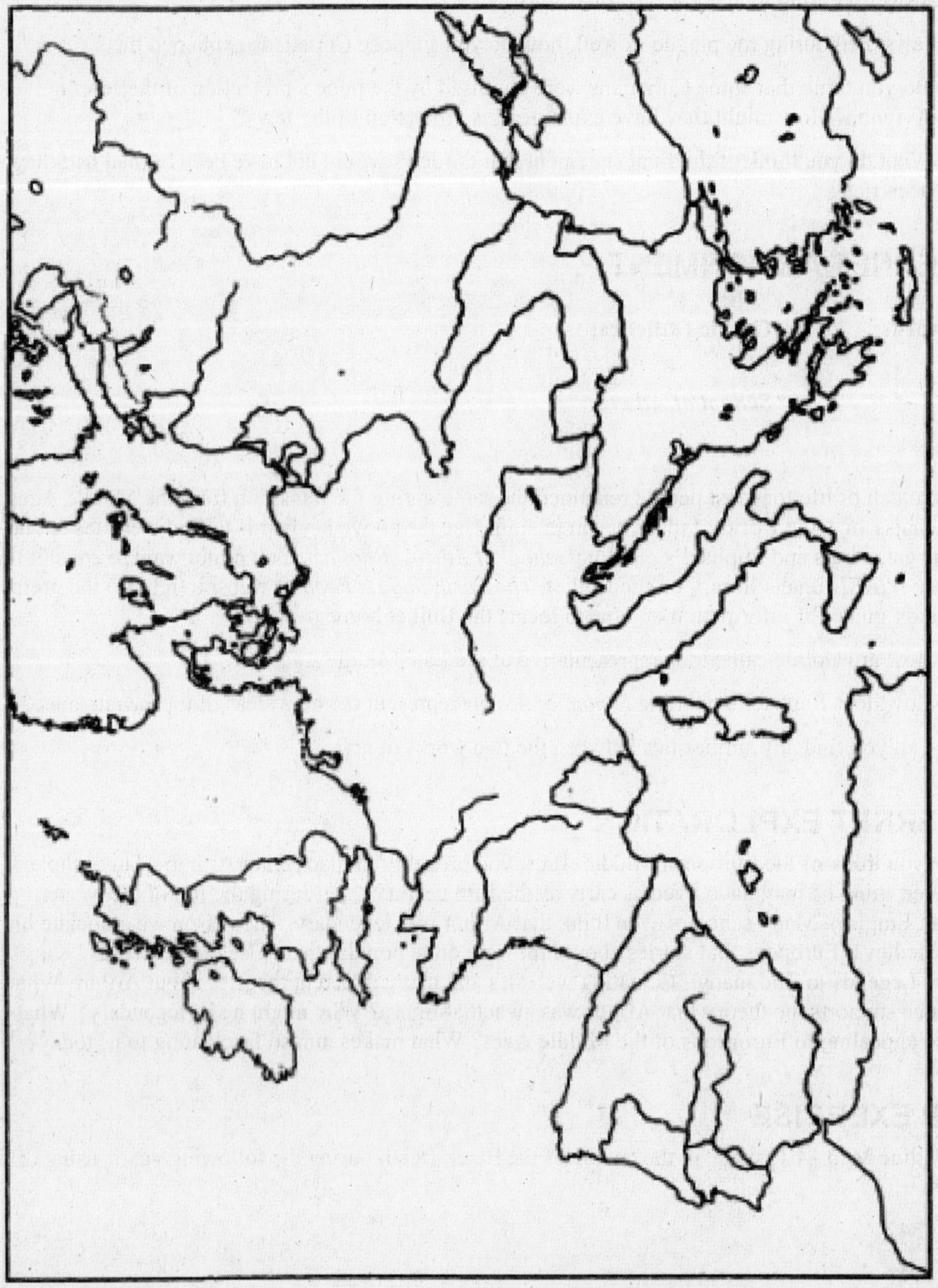

## FOCUS QUESTIONS

1. Trace the growth of European industry, technology, and trade in the Middle Ages through the development of the textile industry.
2. What social, political, and economic role(s) did guilds play?
3. How did Europe benefit from cultural borrowing? From whom did they borrow and what was borrowed?
4. How did the political relationship among monarchs, nobles, and the church change from 1200 to 1500 C.E.?
5. How did European and Japanese feudalism compare (see Chapter 12)?
6. How did the major economic, social, and political elements of Europe change from 1200 to 1500 C.E.?
7. What opportunities and limitations did elite women experience before 1500 C.E. in *two* of the following regions: Europe, Middle East, East Asia (see Chapters 12 and 13)?
8. How did Europe's and sub-Saharan Africa's interaction with the Islamic world compare (see Chapter 13)?

## ANSWERS TO MULTIPLE-CHOICE QUESTIONS

1. e pp. 383–384
2. d p. 385
3. d p. 389
4. b p. 387
5. a p. 387
6. c p. 389
7. a p. 390
8. a p. 395
9. b p. 395
10. b p. 400
11. e p. 400
12. a p. 405

CHAPTER 15

# The Maritime Revolution, to 1550

## BEFORE YOU BEGIN

This chapter begins a new era in world history. Long-distance trade and communication existed long before Columbus, but the degree and consequences of cross-cultural contact increased dramatically from 1400 to 1550 C.E. For the first time, the entire globe (including the Americas) became connected by trade and communication. That may sound like an exaggeration because the degree of contact was minimal by modern standards, but the next several chapters deal directly or indirectly with the consequences of what later came to be known as the Columbian Exchange. Focusing specifically on the state of long-distance trade and exploration around the world before 1450 C.E., this chapter then analyzes how and why Europe changed its attitudes and behavior toward exploration over the next century. Columbus's discovery of the new world is certainly a part of this Age of Exploration, but it is by no means the *only* significant development.

Over the next several chapters, look for long-term trends that explain how and why Europe's relationship to the rest of the world changed so dramatically between 1500 and 1750 C.E. World exploration affected various regions unequally, but that is far different than the common misperception that Europe was somehow the only "active" participant in the process, while other regions were "passive." Historians today look back and summarize this period as the Rise of the West, but at the time it was far from clear that this was happening. Thus, the true importance of 1492 unfolded only slowly and wasn't fully realized until several centuries later.

## LEARNING OBJECTIVES

After reading Chapter 15 and completing this study chapter, you should be able to:

- Discuss in what ways the period from 1400 to 1550 represents a departure from earlier global expansion.
- Identify through what motives and methods Europeans gained global dominance.
- Explain how the peoples of Africa, Asia, and the Americas reacted to European dominance.
- Explain why European empire building was more effective in the Americas than in either Africa or Asia.

## IDENTIFICATIONS

Define each term and explain why it is significant, including any important dates.

**Zheng He**

_______________________________________________

_______________________________________________

**Arawak**

**Henry the Navigator**

**caravel**

**Gold Coast**

**Treaty of Tordesillas**

**Bartolomeu Dias**

**Vasco da Gama**

**Christopher Columbus**

**Ferdinand Magellan**

**Kongo**

**Christian Ethiopia**

**Malacca**

**conquistadors**

**Hernán Cortés**

**Moctezuma II**

**Francisco Pizarro**

**Atahualpa**

## MULTIPLE-CHOICE QUESTIONS

Read the entire question, including *all* the possible answers. Then choose the *one* answer that best fits the question.

1. The *Victoria*'s successful return to Spain in 1522 was
   a. the signal that the Spanish were not to be the dominant force in the Americas.
   b. the crowning example of the Europeans' new ability and determination to make themselves masters of the oceans.
   c. the end of the first expedition led by the English.
   d. the final glory of Spanish dominance in Asia.
   e. confirmation of Magellan's failure.
2. The Polynesian migrations were
   a. obviously accidental since Polynesians lacked navigational devices to plot their way.
   b. obviously from the Americas as Thor Heyerdhal proved in 1947.
   c. the result of a planned expansion.
   d. really a small and unimpressive achievement.
   e. probably really Phoenicians blown off course.

3. Why did the Viking settlements of Greenland and Vinland go into decline after 1200?
   a. The bubonic plague broke out.
   b. Those colonies seceded.
   c. The Vikings' attention was drawn to continental affairs.
   d. The mainland Vikings became Christians, but the island Vikings did not, causing a breach between the two groups.
   e. The weather changed.
4. Which of the following did *not* contribute to the Iberians' decision to begin making the voyages of exploration?
   a. The revival of urban life and trade
   b. The desire to find a route to the Americas
   c. A struggle with Islamic powers for dominance of the Mediterranean
   d. Growing intellectual curiosity about the outside world
   e. An alliance between merchants and rulers
5. The new anti-Muslim Crusades of 1396 and 1444 were launched by the Europeans because
   a. of a renaissance in European Christianity.
   b. the Europeans had finally made contact with the elusive Prester John, and he was going to help reclaim the Holy Land.
   c. the expansion of the Ottoman Turks disrupted trade routes.
   d. they felt the need to compete with the Chinese in their voyages of exploration.
   e. the Ottoman Turks defaulted on their debt to Spain.
6. Which of the following was *not* one aspect of the Portuguese attack on Ceuta in 1415?
   a. A plundering expedition
   b. A religious crusade
   c. A military tournament
   d. A diplomatic overture
   e. An information gathering expedition, particularly to gain knowledge about African caravans
7. Columbus finally persuaded Queen Isabella and King Ferdinand to finance his voyage to the East Indies by
   a. impressing them with his command of geography.
   b. offering a money-back guarantee.
   c. proving his theory by using a ninth-century Arab map.
   d. sheer persistence.
   e. threatening to sail for France.
8. Why did Columbus call the native people of the Americas "Indians"?
   a. He thought that he had landed on an island in the East Indies.
   b. He thought that he had landed in India.
   c. *Indian* means "foreigner."
   d. *Indian* means "savage."
   e. *Indian* means "beloved of God."
9. The Treaty of Tordesillas (1494)
   a. split the world between Spain and Portugal.
   b. legalized African slave trading.
   c. protected Amerindians from Spanish abuses.
   d. was vetoed by the pope.
   e. prevented Brazil from being claimed by Portugal.

10. When the Portuguese first encountered African kingdoms, they
    a. found nothing of interest there.
    b. were equal in power or even less powerful than their African counterparts.
    c. easily dominated them.
    d. found that Africans had no interest in trade.
    e. found that Africans were eager for trade.
11. What finally kept Portugal and Ethiopia from making a permanent alliance?
    a. The Portuguese were afraid to make an alliance with a Muslim kingdom.
    b. Ethiopia needed military assistance that the Portuguese were unwilling to give.
    c. Ethiopia was led by a queen, and Christian countries were never led by female monarchs.
    d. Ethiopia refused to transfer Christian affiliation from the patriarch of Alexandria to the pope in Rome.
    e. The Portuguese discovered that the Ethiopians were plotting against them.
12. The Portuguese were able to assert control over the Indian Ocean because
    a. of the superiority of Christianity over indigenous beliefs.
    b. the constant warfare in the region allowed the disruption of traditional trade systems.
    c. Portuguese trade goods were vastly superior to anything to be found in the region.
    d. of the temporary alliance they were able to make with the Ethiopians.
    e. of the superiority of their ships and weapons over the smaller and lightly armed merchant dhows.
13. How did the Arawaks respond to the Spaniards' ever-increasing demands for gold?
    a. They gladly provided more of their plentiful gold.
    b. They told Columbus exaggerated stories about gold in other places to persuade him to move on.
    c. They ran away.
    d. They held Columbus for ransom in order to get gold from the Spaniards.
    e. They attacked Columbus's fort.
14. Which of the following factors did *not* contribute to the success of the Spanish in creating a vast land empire so quickly in the Americas?
    a. Spaniards immigrated in great numbers to the American colonies.
    b. The long isolation of the Americas made its inhabitants vulnerable to European diseases.
    c. The Spanish had superior military technology.
    d. The Spaniards' used a no-holds-barred fighting style that they learned at home against the Muslims.
    e. The Spaniards had gained a psychological edge from the use of muskets and cannon.
15. Europeans were so much more successful in establishing territorial empires in the Americas than in Africa and Asia for all of the following reasons *except*:
    a. the native populations of the Americas were vulnerable to diseases like smallpox and measles.
    b. the Ottoman navy successfully resisted the advances of Portuguese and Spanish explorers and conquistadors.
    c. most African kingdoms strictly limited European influence to a few port cities, rarely allowing Europeans much contact in the interior of the continent.
    d. the Indian Ocean states had already had contact with the Chinese (Zheng He) whose fleet was much more impressive than the Europeans'.
    e. Indian merchants were already experienced with long-distance trade throughout the Indian Ocean basin.

16. The European explorations and conquests from 1450 to 1550 were most significant because
    a. Europe had not had direct contact with East Asia before this time.
    b. Europe conquered the Americas even more quickly than the Mongols had conquered Asia.
    c. European explorers introduced the slave trade to Africa.
    d. European exploration signaled a new age characterized by growing global interaction.
    e. no previous civilizations had crossed the world's oceans.

## ESSAY QUESTIONS

Make an outline of each question, listing the major points you want to discuss. Then write your practice essay, following your outline carefully and making sure that you do not skip any of your major points. At this time, you will want to add the relevant dates and details that will make your essay persuasive and accurate.

### Change Over Time

1. Briefly describe the non-European patterns of expansion before 1450. What were the goals in these expansions and what methods were used to achieve them?
2. What were the Europeans' motives and methods in their voyages of exploration?
3. Describe the role of the Portuguese in the Indian Ocean trading network. What methods did they use and how successful were they in achieving their goals?

### Compare and Contrast

1. Compare and contrast three responses to European exploration.
2. Why were Europeans so much more successful in establishing territorial empires in the Americas than in Africa and Asia?
3. Compare Ming China's and Europe's attitudes and actions toward exploration from 1400 to 1550 C.E.

## COMPARISON CHARTS

Using information gathered from the text, fill in the blank areas of each chart with the relevant data pertaining to the regions and categories listed. (Not all blank areas will necessarily be equally complete.)

Chart 15.1

PATTERNS OF EXPANSION

| | Dates | Regions | Goals | Technology | Impact |
|---|---|---|---|---|---|
| Spanish/Portuguese | | | | | |
| Mongol | | | | | |
| Chinese | | | | | |
| Muslim | | | | | |
| Malaysian-Indonesian | | | | | |
| Amerindian | | | | | |

Chart 15.2

**EUROPEAN IMPACT IN ASIA AND AFRICA VERSUS IMPACT IN AMERICA**

| | Asia/Africa | America |
|---|---|---|
| **Motives** | | |
| **Methods** | | |
| **Response by Local Peoples** | | |

## DIVERSITY AND DOMINANCE

After reading "Diversity and Dominance: Congo's Christian King" in your text, answer the following additional questions.

1. How do you think people respond to unfamiliar and frightening cultures? Put yourself in the place of Moctezuma; how would you see the Spanish?
2. Why is it so important that Juan Ginés de Sepúlveda need to demonstrate the barbarity of the Amerindians? Do you see similarities between the two cultures?

## INTERNET ASSIGNMENT

**Keywords:** **Psalter world map**

**Henricus Martellus map** or **Cantino world map**

Maps are valuable tools we use to locate streets, schools, and vacation spots. But maps can also be used to learn about the people who created them. Use the above keywords to locate websites about the Psalter world map, Henricus Martellus map, and the Cantino world map. You might want to consult the *History WIRED* image library on the Bulliet, *The Earth and Its Peoples* website (refer to the preface of this study guide for information on how to locate the Bulliet home page). The first keyword is for a map from the Middle Ages, and the second set of keywords is for maps from the early Renaissance period.

1. What do you notice about the map from the Middle Ages? What is missing?
2. How do the Renaissance maps differ in style and geography from the medieval maps?
3. What seems to be the major concern of each map?
4. What do you think of the geographical accuracy of these maps?
5. How does each map reflect the outlook of the people who created them?

## INTERNET EXPLORATION

Today, with modern jets, satellites, and transatlantic conference calls, it's hard to imagine that long, dangerous voyages were once the only way to see the world. But in the sixteenth century, the only way to travel was on wooden oceangoing vessels with uncertain navigational techniques. To learn something about how we used to travel, use the keywords "Spanish caravel." Would you like to have been alive in those days, sailing into unknown lands? What adventures and perils might you have encountered?

## MAP EXERCISES

On Outline Map 15.1, plot the routes of the following:

- Voyages of Zheng He
- Polynesian voyages
- Malaysian-Indonesian voyages
- African voyages
- Prince Henry the Navigator's ships
- Christopher Columbus
- Vasco Da Gama
- Amerigo Vespucci
- Ferdinand Magellan

On Outline Map 15.2, use shading to differentiate the following:

- Aztec Empire
- Inca Empire
- Arawak homeland
- Arawak voyages
- Carib voyages
- Andean voyages

## Outline Map 15.1

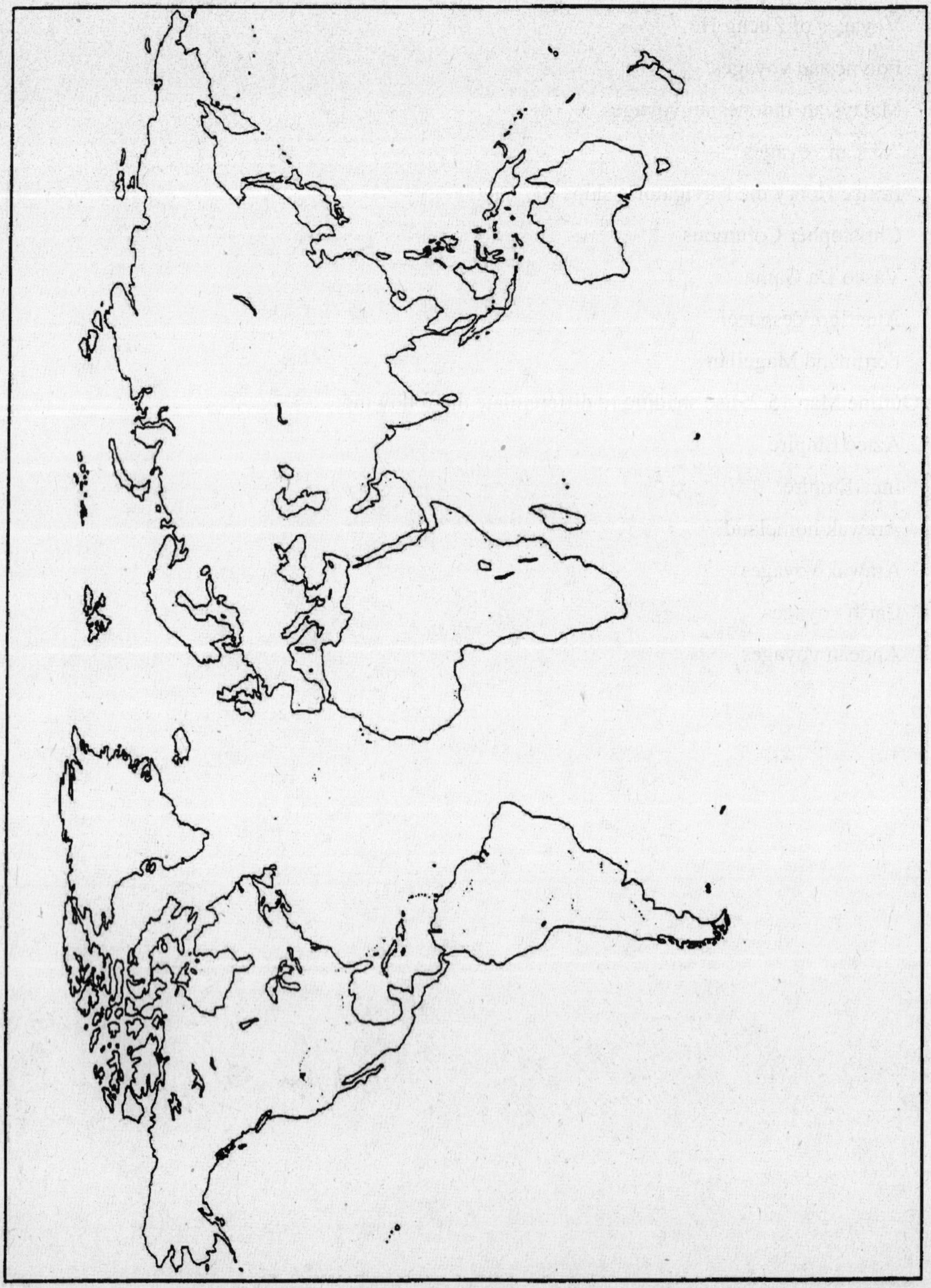

## Outline Map 15.2

## FOCUS QUESTIONS

1. What developments make 1500 a major turning point in world history? How are the years after 1500 different from the preceding years?
2. What factors enabled European countries to begin a new age of global exploration and conquest around 1500 C.E.?
3. How did Europe's attitudes and actions toward exploration compare with Ming China's from 1400 to 1550 C.E.?

## ANSWERS TO MULTIPLE-CHOICE QUESTIONS

1. b p. 412
2. c p. 414
3. e p. 417
4. b p. 418
5. c p. 419
6. d p. 419
7. d p. 423
8. a p. 424
9. a p. 424
10. e p. 425
11. d p. 427
12. e p. 427
13. b p. 431
14. a pp. 432–433
15. b p. 425
16. d p. 417